D0366022

Education for *Life*

Preparing Children to Meet the Challenges

Education for *Life*

Preparing Children to Meet the Challenges

by J. Donald Walters

Crystal

Clarity

Crystal Clarity, Publishers
14618 Tyler-Foote Road
Nevada City, CA 95959
800-424-1055

Copyright © 1986, 1997 by J. Donald Walters

All rights reserved

Cover painting by Oliver Graf
Cover and book design by Christine Starner Schuppe

First printing, 1986
Revised edition, 1997

Printed in the United States of America

ISBN: 1-56589-740-4

1 3 5 7 9 8 6 4 2

Crystal

Clarity

Crystal Clarity, Publishers
14618 Tyler-Foote Road
Nevada City, CA 95959
800-424-1055
http://www.consciousnet.com/CrystalClarity

Contents

Introduction

For twenty years I have served in various roles as teacher, guidance counselor, principal, college instructor, and consultant in public education. During that time I have participated in experimental projects for educational change, seen theories of education come and go, and read most of the current books on educational reform.

Among all the books I have read, *Education for Life* stands out as that rare pedagogical phenomenon: a book both refreshingly original and wholly workable.

Education for Life expands the current definition of schooling; it offers parents, educators, and concerned citizens everywhere techniques for transforming education into an integral process—one which harmonizes book learning with direct life experience.

This book recommends an already tested and proven system of education, one which emphasizes relevancy when teaching the "basics," and instructs children also in the art of living. As Walters states, this book has the further goal of helping people to ". . . see the whole of life, beyond the years that one spends in school, as education."

The unique perspective offered by the author will, I think, give his readers a sense of discovery. Walters has taken seemingly difficult concepts, and offered simple definitions for them that are as convincing as they are unexpected. For example, he defines that seemingly vague word, maturity, as "the ability to relate appropriately to other realities than one's own." Immaturity he defines as "a little child throwing a tantrum on the floor because he can't get what he wants." Definitions like these stand out both for their simple clarity, and because they are exceptionally helpful. Parents and teachers will readily recognize them as being right on target!

Another thing I liked about this book: While profound, it is at the same time enjoyable to read!

Education for Life deserves to be read by dreamers and doers alike. Perhaps even dreamers, after reading it, will put it to use! For it offers direction for those people who feel that education should mean more than an acquisition of facts, more than intellectual exposure to a vast number of untested concepts, and more than a pragmatic preparation for employment. It is an exalted call for change, based on deep insight into the potentials of every human being. It tells us how to nurture creativity, wisdom, and intuition in each child, and how to tap his unexplored capabilities.

Jesse J. Casbon, Ph.D., Dean
Graduate School for Professional Studies
Lewis & Clark College
Portland, Oregon

Preface

The title of this book can be understood in two ways, both of them intentionally so. Primarily, my purpose has been to recommend a system of education that will prepare children for meeting life's challenges, and not only fit them for employment or for intellectual pursuits. I have also wanted, however, to help the reader to see the whole of life, beyond the years spent in school, as education.

For if indeed, as most people deeply believe, life has purpose and meaning, then its goal must be to educate us ever-more fully to that meaning. And the true goal of the education we receive during our school years must be to help prepare us for that lifelong learning process.

Chapter 1

Success Is Achieving What One REALLY Wants

Have you a growing child? If no , suppose you had one: What would you like him or her to become? A doctor? lawyer? scientist? business executive? or, if a girl who hopes for marriage instead of a career, the *wife* of one of these?

Most people want their children to have certain basic advantages: prosperity, a good job, the respect of their fellow human beings. Too often, unfortunately, their ambitions stop there. They are centered in materialistic, not in spiritual, values.

Systems of education are directed largely by what parents want for their children. Because most parents want material advantages for them, the modern system of education was developed primarily with this goal in mind. Little attention, if any, has been paid to helping students to become *successful human beings*.

How far might the present philosophy of education be carried?

I once read about a Mafia capo who was kissed worshipfully on the back of his hand by a poor peasant woman in Sicily—not, it seems, for any favor he had done her, and certainly not in admiration for his character. Why, then, would she demonstrate such adulation? One can only assume it was because his thefts and murders had brought him great material power. And what mattered the sick conscience which must have been his own constant companion? That, apparently, in the woman's eyes, was *his* problem. To her, anyway, and probably to many others, the man deserved admiration because he had achieved worldly power.

We've all heard of, and perhaps also met, wealthy people of dubious character who were more or less excused their "eccentricities" solely on account of their wealth.

But do riches really constitute success? Surely not, and especially not if, in the process, the admiration they attract is mingled with general dislike. What is it, to succeed at the cost of one's own happiness and peace of mind, and at the cost of other people's sincere respect and good will?

Success means much more than money and power. Of what good are millions of dollars, if their attainment deprives one of all that makes life truly worth living? Many people have learned this lesson too late in life to have any time left to improve matters. Why then—they may have wondered belatedly—were they encouraged in the first place so to distort their values?

For, of course, they *were* encouraged. Everything they ever learned at home, in school, and from their peers persuaded them that success lies in things tangible, not in seemingly insubstantial, more spiritual gains.

It comes down to what people *really* want from life. Doesn't the object of this desire lie beyond such tangible acquisitions as money, prestige, and power? They want these for the inner satisfaction, the happiness, they expect to gain through them. It is self-evident, then, that what people really want from life is not the mere symbols of happiness, but happiness itself.

Why, then, don't our schools teach students not only how to be successful materially, but successful also as people? I'm not saying that dusty facts such as the dates of trade embargoes and ententes may not serve a useful purpose also. But why don't our schools teach, in addition to those facts, skills more clearly focused on human needs and interests, such as how to get along well with others, and, even more importantly, how to get along with *oneself?* how to live healthfully? how to concentrate? how to develop one's latent abilities? how to be a good employee, or a good boss? how to find a suitable mate? how to have a harmonious home life? how to acquire balance in one's life?

Few mathematics teachers try to show their students how the principles of mathematics might help them in the exercise of everyday logic, and of common sense.

Few English teachers try to instill in their students a respect for grammar as a gateway to clear thinking.

Few science teachers bother to show their students how they might apply what they learn in the classroom to creative problem-solving in daily life.

Facts—give them facts! that is the cry. Cram as much data as possible into their perspiring heads in the hope that, if the student has any common sense left in him by the time he graduates, he'll know what to do with that mountain of information he's been forced to ingest during his undergraduate years.

This tendency to confuse knowledge with wisdom becomes a habit for the rest of most people's lives. Seldom has there been a more fact-gathering society than ours is today. And seldom has simple, down-to-earth wisdom been held in lower esteem. One's most casual utterances must be backed by a wealth of statistics, and supported by as many quotations as possible from the words and opinions of others, for one's own utterances to receive even a hearing.

Because our society equates education and wisdom itself with mere knowledge, and because we see this accumulation of knowledge as the be-all and end-all of education, we fail to recognize life for the opportunity, the very adventure, that it is: the opportunity to develop ourselves to our full potential *as human beings;* and the adventure of discovering hitherto unknown facets of our own selves.

Chapter 2

Education Should Be Experiential, Not Merely Theoretical

You've heard that familiar, but time-dishonored, rationalization: "The end justifies the means." Everyone knows that this saying has been offered by "true believers" in multitudes of causes as justification for their violent deeds. A bad tree, however, as Jesus Christ pointed out, produces bad fruit. Evil means lead to evil ends.

And yet—suppose we restate that saying another way, thus: "The end *tests the validity* of the means"? To this statement, no one could object. For only by the actual outcome of a course of action can we verify whether the action was valid or not.

Human deeds justify, or condemn, themselves by their consequences. A man may campaign for peace, yet parade about so angrily in his "peace demonstrations" that all he accomplishes in the end is the disruption of everybody's peace, including his own. A nation may see no harm in destroying its forests to get wood, but the consequences of the act will demonstrate that great harm was done to the ecology. In this case, the end—obtaining wood for fireplaces and for the construction of houses—clearly did not justify the means used. On the other side, if Fulton was ridiculed for building a ship made of metal, the fact that it floated once it was launched was all the justification he needed for his invention.

A course of action is justified if its results are consistently good. It is in the consequences of a theory, similarly, that the theory itself can be justified.

We see here a basic weakness of modern education: It is theoretical, primarily. It places all too little emphasis on practicality. Far from trying to justify any means in terms of their actual results, educators seem to view any concern with the *practical* effects of a theory as a kind of betrayal of the true, scholarly spirit.

I am reminded of the case of a man of only grade school education, but of wide experience in mining engineering, who, late in his life, decided to get a formal education. After great effort he succeeded in persuading the authorities of a university to accept him on the strength of his years of practical experience in the field. A few months later, however, he dropped his studies.

"What have you done?" demanded the dean. "It was so important to you to get an education, and we, too, went to great lengths to get you admitted."

"An education!" the man snorted. "There isn't one of these pedagogues who isn't teaching what I myself learned better in the field. Many of them learned everything they know from *me!* What can they teach me?"

It is no accident, surely, that many of the world's greatest men and women—scientists, thinkers, teachers, molders of public opinion—either never finished their formal education or did poorly in school. Einstein's teachers marked him for a failure in life. Edison could only manage three months of formal schooling, at the end of which his teacher sent him home with a note saying he was "unteachable"—in fact, "addled." Goethe found little worth assimilating during his formal schooling. In fact, he later claimed not to have found a single university course that could hold his interest.

What is the difference between great human beings and the pedagogues who explain their lives and discoveries to others? It is this, quite simply: True greatness focuses on reality, but the explainers get their knowledge and belief systems from books *about* reality. The way-showers of humanity have specific ends in mind—the truth about something, usually— and are committed to achieving those ends by the means most practical for attaining them. They are impatient with attitudes that seem to imply that the means are an end in themselves; that method is more important than results, and that no conclusion is ever final and should always, therefore, be considered tentative. For the pedagogue, on the other hand, theories hold such a fascination that the very intricacy of reasoning in their formulation often replaces the need for arriving at any firm conclusion.

However full a student's head is crammed with book learning, his understanding of things, and of life in general, after twelve or sixteen years of education, is completely unrelated to actual experience. Still less is it the product of self-understanding.

Were we, on the other hand, to define education primarily in terms of what *life* has to teach us, we would soon find reality directing our theories, instead of theories molding our perceptions. But students are seduced into championing hare-brained, and even dangerous, beliefs, all because their teachers are too "objective" to mind if a theory offends against normal human sensibilities and the most rudimentary common sense, as long as it is presented in an attractive wrapping of intellectual reasoning.

Take the teachings of Jean Paul Sartre on the subject of meaninglessness. Sartre was a nihilist. Because he developed his theories brilliantly, they are offered at universities as standard intellectual fare. "The ego is flattered," Paramhansa Yogananda wrote, "that it can grasp such complexity."

A recent survey of professors found that the majority preferred wordy, intellectually intricate and abstruse articles on subjects in their own fields over articles that made the same points, but in a style that was simple and easy to read.

The people conducting the survey then took articles that had been written simply and clearly, and restated them in convoluted terms, replacing short words with long ones wherever possible, and clear statements with others that were muddy or contrived. They offered these altered articles to the same professors, along with the original versions, and asked for a comparative evaluation. Most of those learned peda-gogues, never guessing that they were in essence reading the same article to which not a thought had been added, and from which none had been deleted, declared they preferred the more complex version. When asked why, they replied that the more intel-lectual-sounding version showed better research, deeper thought, and greater insight.

It can be astonishing, the extent to which theories learned during the formative years can direct a person's later perceptions of reality. Any error learned early distorts the very way one reasons. False premises lead to false conclusions no matter how clever the line of reasoning. Theories imposed on reality are allowed to pose as substitutes for the reality itself.

We see this tendency in psychologists who insist, in defiance of their own direct experience, that the mind of a newborn baby is a blank slate on which environment will write the impressions that will form his personality. Nothing in objective reality supports this theory. Parents know how very different, from birth, each child is from all the others. Never mind. Theory says it *should* be so: Therefore, it *is* so.

We see the same tendency in Freud, who adopted virtually as his mission the attempt to explain *all* human motivation in terms of the sex drive. (I can imagine physicists trying to fit Freud's theory to their attempts to discover the laws inherent in quantum mechanics!)

Educated people, far more so than those who have been raised in the "school of hard knocks"—that is to say, of common sense—are notoriously prone to prefer theory over reality.

For education to prepare children for meeting life realistically, it should encourage them to learn from life itself, and to view with skepticism a body of fixed knowledge that has been passed on unquestioned from one generation to the next.

Education must above all be experiential, and not merely theoretical. The student should be taught, among other things, to observe the outcome of any course of action, and not to depend blindly on the claims of others as to what that outcome is supposed to be, and therefore *will* be.

In this simple emphasis on direct experience, not only as regards the investigations of science, but even more so as it applies to the humanities, lie the seeds of a new and revolutionary system of education that I have named here *Education for Life.*

Chapter 3

Reason Must Be Balanced by Feeling

Galileo one day observed the swinging of the great candelabra in the cathedral of Pisa. His reflections on that movement led to his discovery of the law of pendular motion.

Newton one day observed the fall of an apple. It was this observation (according to Voltaire) that led to Newton's discovery of the law of gravity.

All science is discovery. And the glory of the scientific method is that, shunning a priori assumptions, it insists on observing and learning from things *as they are*. The true scientist tries never to impose his expectations on objective reality.

That everyone has expectations, and that these expectations do sometimes impose themselves, unsuspected, on even the work of scientists, should go without saying. Einstein and Sir Arthur Stanley Eddington, both great physicists, were in disagreement on some obscure point of science. Einstein settled the matter by declaring that it was, after all, "only a matter of taste."

Scientists are human. We should not be dismayed if sometimes we even find them out there in the pit of competition, slugging away with the best.

What *is* dismaying is the widespread assumption that, if one can only train oneself to adopt a completely scientific outlook, he will rise altogether above human feeling, and that, in his cold objectivity, he will achieve superior understanding—as though, in that unfeeling state, he could become some kind of intellectual superman. According to this view, human nature is an obstacle, not an aid, to understanding.

It is no accident that so many fictional glimpses into the future portray a world stripped of such "superficial nonsense" as beauty, kindness, happiness, and—probably the first of all to go—humor. Science fiction, a prime example of this genre of literature, can be depressingly sterile. The earth hundreds of years from now is envisioned as a place without trees (at least, none are mentioned), without grass and streams and singing birds; a place where science has finally collared Nature and made her sit down and behave herself. We are offered a supposedly ideal world of steel and new, ultra-strong plastics, of efficient laboratories and smoothly functioning machines—including altogether machinelike human beings.

A famous psychology professor made a practice of telling his first-year students, "If anyone here thinks he has a soul, please park it outside the classroom before entering." (This cute remark of course won him the smug titters he was fishing for.) What he was actually telling his students was, in effect, "We're going to approach our subject with intellectual objectivity—scientifically, and without any human pretensions." And what he achieved was another shovelful of dirt onto the coffin of Keats's famous dictum—passé, alas, nowadays—"Truth is beauty; beauty, truth."

For what the "good" professor was also saying was, To be scientific, we psychologists have a duty to view human nature as the physicist views matter—as a thing, merely: a collection of molecules, conscious only because matter, in the long, meandering process of evolution, happened to produce a brain.

In this view of human nature, it is of course absurd to postulate a soul.

In such a case, however, it is equally absurd to suppose ideals, to encourage fantasy, to reach *upward* toward anything at all. This view encourages us to remain satisfied with reaching *down* toward the merely "gut-level" satisfactions of instinctual, animal desires.

Sri Radhakrishnan, formerly the vice president of India, said during the conversation I once had with him, "A nation is known by the men and women it looks up to as great." In light of his remark, rich in the simplicity of wisdom, does it not seem at times as though the model we are being offered today of the ideal human being were something akin to a robot?

In how many modern novels do we find the hero described as smoothly efficient, unemotional, finely tooled physically and mentally—indeed, machinelike. For these qualities we are expected—not to *like* him, perhaps (that would be asking too much), but at any rate to admire him.

When intellectuality is not balanced with feelings, it can produce a Hamlet complex, thereby paralyzing action. Too many professors, with the claim of objectivity, betray their bias against commitment of any kind. How different they are in this respect from the truly great scientists of our age.

Einstein claimed that the essence of scientific inquiry is a sense of mystical awe before the wonders of the universe. Great scientists generally, like most great human beings, are dreamers as well as people of action. And they are *committed* to their dreams—their vision, if you will. One thinks here of Edison testing 43,000 filaments before finding one that would work in an incandescent light bulb. His assistants, after some 20,000 experiments, pleaded with him to abandon the quest. Imagine such extraordinary commitment to what seemed to everyone else an impossible dream!

And how different the great scientist, in this respect, from the average pedagogue, who represents the scientist's discoveries in the classroom! More or less forgotten, by the time the scientist's life and findings are included in textbooks, is his enthusiasm, his total commitment to his subject.

It seems likely that the pedagogues, fearful as they are of intellectual commitment, are partly responsible for the frozen image so many people hold nowadays of the ideal human being. Our school system breeds preoccupation with mere things, and with abstract ideas, while fostering indifference to values that are more closely human.

Psychology itself, however, tells us that human feelings cannot be suppressed. Ignore a person's emotional life instead of trying to develop it along constructive lines, and those emotions will simply find other, and often destructive, outlets for self-expression.

Unfortunately, psychologists have also encouraged the unbridled expression of emotions as a means of ridding oneself of them. They don't discuss how to refine the emotions. Emotions themselves are viewed merely as obstacles to understanding. Thus, people have been led to believe that the way to find release from their feelings is to give them free rein.

Consider television—that mirror of public attitudes and opinions. One has only to turn on the television set to be confronted (within a few minutes) with examples of almost embarrassing immaturity. Screams of anger, gratuitous insults, kicks and fisticuffs, a refusal to listen to the simplest common sense, even shooting at others—such behavior is presented as perfectly normal. Selfish indifference to the needs of others is taken quite for granted. No suggestion is offered that calm, refined feelings are the true norm for mature human behavior, and that disturbed emotions are an aberration of that norm; that, although the emotions can distort a person's perceptions of reality, *refined* emotions, in the form of pure feeling, can clarify those perceptions. The intellect is one of the tools provided by Nature for accessing her secrets. Feeling, however, when calm, is the other tool. Of the two, feeling is the more important.

The West, in its scientific achievements, has much to be proud of. After a life of traveling around the world, however, I wonder whether Western civilization isn't also producing people of stunted psychological and spiritual development.

I am reminded of an answer given by Mahatma Gandhi to the question, "What do you think of Western civilization?" With a wry smile he replied, "I think it would be a good idea!"

Science has provided an important key to the advancement of knowledge by insisting that no belief system be imposed on our perceptions of objective Nature. Nothing in this scientific approach need limit us to material research alone. We must listen, rather, to *whatever* Nature has to tell us, going beyond belief even in matters of spiritual development, and strive always to harmonize ourselves with whatever *is*.

Science has taught us to learn from Nature. Why not, then, seek to learn from *human* nature, and also from divine nature?

This process may not be rightly the task of our school system any more than scientific discoveries themselves are expected in the classrooms. The purpose of schooling is to pass on to students what has been learned already in the great school of life. Much has been learned already, however, about human and divine nature through the millennia. Many discoveries have been made also regarding the search for true fulfillment in life. A good start in the schools, then, would be to include among the subjects covered in the classroom an intelligent study of these findings.

The need, moreover, is to approach these findings with the same objectivity that true science has shown—not *cold,* intellectual objectivity, merely, but the objectivity also of calm feeling.

From life only can lessons be drawn that have repeatedly, in the past, shown human beings the ways to better living.

Chapter 4

How Progressive, Really, Is "Progressive"?

Abstract theories are more the subject of university than of grade school education. The *effect* of those theories, however, is widely apparent even in teaching at the grade school level.

There are few areas in life so susceptible to dogmatism—indeed, even to bigotry and the denunciation of alien views as "heresies"—than child education. And there are few dogmas so persistent as the belief in a child's "natural" wisdom. This belief is somewhat akin to Rousseau's "noble savage," an imaginary creature if ever there was one, but one in whom many people fervently believed.

Yes, of course children sometimes display astonishing insights. Most of us have marveled at the depth of understanding revealed by them. "Natural man," too, because of his very lack of sophistication, knows many things that become lost in the civilizing process. There is much indeed that both primitive peoples and children have to teach us. But this state of affairs stops far short of the next point many adults like to make—namely, that children ought to determine what they themselves need to learn.

"Progressive" education, as it was named several decades ago, has been in many ways a step away from order and common sense, and toward chaos.

I don't intend to deal here with the issue of discipline vs. permissiveness, though that is certainly one problem that permissive education raises. But what I want to emphasize is how important to the term "progressive" is the simple concept, *progression.*

It seems obvious that the learning process should take one from *somewhere* to *something:* from relative ignorance to relative understanding. One can't begin with the poetic assumption that it is the adult, really, who needs educating, though it's the sort of statement that draws approving nods around a campfire.

I heard a popular writer once address a large audience with the statement, "I don't know what I'm doing up here [on the platform]. *You all* should be up here teaching me! And I should be down there, listening to you."

"Come off it!" I thought. "If you really mean what you're saying, why don't you just get down here with the rest of us and have done with it?" He was posturing, merely; he knew he was committed to being up there. For one thing, he was being paid to speak.

We all know, of course—if we aren't too lost in our dogmas—that the child will sooner or later have to study the "three *r*s" ("'readin', 'ritin', an' 'rithmetic"). Children aren't born with this knowledge. In the field of moral, religious, and social values, however, the coast is clear for complete dominance by the "progressive" method of education.

"We don't want to impose our own values on our children!" goes the cry. "Children know what is right for them. Let *them* decide what they should believe." Does this mean, then, that all belief systems are matters of mere conjecture? Well, no; no one says that. To believe in the "belief systems" of science, for example, is acceptable. But why not, then, in the findings of people who are known to have lived their lives wisely?

Many interesting "laws of life" have appeared in recent times: Murphy's Law, Parkinson's Law, and the Peter Principle, to name a few. In keeping with this pleasant tradition I'd like (tongue-in-cheek) to propose another law called "Walters' Law of Dogmatic Proliferation"—my little "float," as it were, in the parade: *The weight of dogmatism increases in inverse proportion to that of the evidence people offer in its support.*

It is in the less fact-centered subjects that dogmatism proliferates, a proliferation that sometimes reaches the point of outright fanaticism. We find the fanaticism most pronounced in politics and religion, but education comes in a close third. Rousseau's "noble savage" has been replaced in modern educational theories by the "noble child." The only strong discouragement such a child receives from following his own "natural" bent is, I understand, a sign that is posted in many high school corridors: "No guns. No drugs."

Meanwhile, man's ethical development fails increasingly to keep abreast of his scientific advancement. At present, the human race stands in imminent danger of bombing itself back to the caves—or to heaven, or wherever.

Are our children really qualified to teach us the secrets we need to know for our survival as a species? That little toddler whom we may imagine lisping pleadingly, "Mommy, please, please love Daddy! Oh, Daddy, *please* give Mommy a kiss!" may indeed have chalked up some small victory for international peace, but his victory is just as likely to receive a set-back a few moments later, when he screams at his little sister, "Give me back my toy!"

Imagining children to be already fully aware regarding basic issues of behavior and belief, we let them grow up without guidance in these crucial matters. Later on in life, we may wonder why so many of them remain emotionally immature and without faith in anything or anyone.

The very educative process, especially in high school and college, is so directed as to strip a child of any faith he may once have had.

For example, one of the dogmas of modern thought, presented with smug self-satisfaction in the university classrooms as a sign of the teacher's "objectivity," is the belief, supposedly drawn from science, that life has no meaning. This message is presented subtly, of course, but our youths get the message, and it filters down even to the youngsters in grade school. The evolution of man, they learn, is the product of a long series of "sports" of nature. Everything is relative, moreover: moral values, spiritual "verities," political systems.

Says who? Not Einstein, certainly.

Einstein himself wasn't thinking of these things when he proclaimed the speed of light as the only "absolute" in physics. Philosophers, however, quickly applied Einsteinian relativity to moral and spiritual values also. It was one thing for a physicist to relate material phenomena to the constant speed of light, but quite another for philosophers, claiming physics as their justification, to claim that, all things being relative, no absolute truths exist. What kind of thinking is this? The physicist has at least *something* as a constant. Philosophers of relativity have given us nothing.

In line with this new thinking, children are taught that evolution is not progressive, since there is nowhere for it to progress to; that it might just as easily, in other words, have reached an alternative pinnacle in some kind of mammalian dinosaur, stupid but invincible, as it did in the present rulers of the earth, the human race. As one psychologist put it rhetorically, "Has mankind evolved more in producing a brain than the elephant in producing a trunk?" To that writer the answer was self-evident: No.

With all the modern emphasis on meaninglessness, the best we seem to have been able to give our children has been the conviction that there is no real purpose to anything, so they may as well fend for themselves. (Why should we do the fending for them? Of course, we must dress that thought up in elegant clothing. "Give them the *freedom,*" we say, "to fend for themselves.") This is an intellectual dogma of our times, and the dogmatism with which its proponents declare it increases, as I've said, in direct proportion to their inability to convert people of common sense to their view. But we mustn't be too surprised if, in consequence, our children retaliate in anger against this supposed state of affairs.

A growing child needs faith just as urgently as he needs air to breathe. When he is stripped of his last vestige of faith, his disillusionment transforms itself into a desire for vengeance against those who have deprived him of something so precious to his very existence.

Teachers talk long and patiently about the need for objectivity. But is it objectivity their pupils actually acquire in the process? They are taught to sneer at subjectivity as a mark of bias and emotionalism ("We mustn't make 'value judgments'"), but how much has really been accomplished in the process? After doing their best to deny their own emotions, they find those emotions surfacing in wholly irrational ways.

That delightful children's fantasy, *The Never-Ending Story,* makes an important point: When fantasy is suppressed, it resurfaces in the form of lies. Emotions suppressed, similarly, reduce a person's ability to cope realistically with life.

What then? Surely it is time we kept scientific abstraction in its place, and recognized that there are other rooms in this house of earthly experience that need furnishing also. I don't at all mean to drive science out of the building: Its place is important. But let us keep science, and the scientific method, in their proper place, and not invite them to decide everything that goes on in the other rooms.

It is axiomatic, surely, that our children's upbringing ought to be progressive, in the sense of leading them *somewhere.* Where, then, should it lead? Leaving abstractions aside, isn't the simple, obvious, most basic answer this: to lead them from immaturity to maturity? Isn't the attainment of maturity what growing up is really all about?

If so, then it becomes necessary to ask ourselves, What *is* maturity?

For an answer, let me offer you another law, "The Maturity Principle": *Maturity is the ability to relate appropriately to other realities than one's own.*

*Im*maturity is self-evidently displayed in the opposite kind of behavior. Immaturity is a little child throwing a temper tantrum in a public mall because he can't get what he wants. Children discover as they grow up that life isn't always disposed to comply with their wishes. The process of growing up is one of learning to "play the odds"—to adapt to situations *as they are,* and not as one wishes they were. Immature people typically decry such adaptation as "compromise," though the compromise need be no greater than Edison's was to the necessity for conducting thousands of experiments to find a filament that could light an incandescent bulb.

Many people learn to dissemble their frustration when their hopes are disappointed, but not many learn how to banish frustration altogether. They mature a little, but not much, beyond the child with his temper tantrums. Much might have been accomplished during the time they were growing up to cure them of this infantilism. Instead, the very dogmas of our times feed their immaturity instead of curing it.

Not long ago, during an economic recession in Detroit, many hundreds of workers had to be laid off. A considerable number of them were given psychiatric counseling to help them adjust to their predicament. There were too many such cases, however, to make this counseling available to everyone. Interestingly, it turned out that those who were given counseling had a notably more difficult time adjusting to their new circumstances than those who were given none.

How to explain these unexpected results? The report said that the "beneficiaries" of counseling were hindered from simply getting on with it. Instead, they were encouraged to dwell on their predicament, to "see it objectively," and to consider various theoretical means of coping with it. Those who missed the opportunity for counseling wasted no time in theorizing about their misfortune, and set themselves instead to simply doing what had to be done to rebuild their lives.

Maturity is not a finishing line reached automatically at a certain age. It is a continuous—even a never-ending—process. Who, indeed, may claim that there are no levels of reality to which he still needs to learn to relate? Who knows where our ultimate horizons lie? We sail toward an ever-receding horizon of awareness until at last it turns out to be a complete circle, expanding outward to infinity.

This book is directed toward helping children to find their way *progressively* toward maturity. My assumption throughout, then, is that maturity is a basic goal for *all* human beings. It is not the goal only of formal education. Education for life continues throughout all the years of our lives.

Chapter 5

Every Child's Real Self

"Gnothi sauton," proclaimed the inscription at the oracle of Delphi: "Know thyself."

"The proper study of mankind," wrote Alexander Pope, "is man."

"This above all," stated Shakespeare through the mouth of Polonius in *Hamlet,* "to thine own self be true."

How many times have great minds offered mankind the counsel to "turn within" in the quest for wisdom. Man's very ability to relate meaningfully to others depends first of all on his own sensitivity. As Shakespeare put it again (concluding the above quote), "And it shall follow as the day the night, thou canst not then be false to any man."

It is this eternal truth—this *wisdom*—that has been swept aside in the modern rush for more "scientific" values. And yet, even scientific discovery has not been granted to every scientist. We see that, in certain respects at least, the greatest scientists have also been great human beings—not great merely because of their brilliance, but in a fuller and deeper sense. Indeed, intelligence alone is a very poor criterion of greatness. There are far too many intelligent idiots in this world, who show a regrettable lack of common sense despite their intelligence.

Great scientists demonstrate greatness also in their ability to rise above petty self-preoccupation and reach out toward broader realities. Lesser scientists generally,

34

like lesser human beings everywhere, have not shown even an inclination in this direction.

Motivation is only one test of greatness. Lesser scientists, and lesser human beings generally, are almost by definition motivated by the thought, "What's in it for me? What will *I* get out of it?" It is their pettiness that makes them lesser. The broader the outlook on life, the less the concern with personal gain. Admittedly, there have been great scientists as well as great people in other fields who, owing to egotism or personal ambition, were less great than they might have been. In their work at least, however, they were able—far better than most people—to rise above pettiness. Often, indeed, it was their high energy that passed in the minds of little people for egotism.

Great scientists, again, have been clear and calm enough in themselves to be able to focus all their energy and attention on the tasks at hand. Most people lack this ability to concentrate. They haven't, therefore, that extra faculty of perception which is the final secret of genius. Sensitive perception is a natural product of calm concentration. Another word for it is intuition.

Luther Burbank, the famous botanist, was so inwardly focused during his experiments with plants that his eyes would often remain half closed and half open, gazing inwardly as much as outwardly. Other botanists of his day challenged his findings on the basis that they hadn't been able to duplicate them. Yet the new botanical strains he produced sufficiently proved the reality of his discoveries.

Burbank considered self-knowledge an essential part of the work he did with plants. Who can say whether even insight into the workings of the cosmos doesn't require, first, a degree of self-knowledge?

Pythagoras, the Greek sage, lived at a time when civilized man had neither the facts nor the vision to think of the universe as anything but flat, and geocentric. Yet Pythagoras stated that the Earth is round, and that we and all the visible stars revolve around a great central fire. His explanation of things, for many centuries considered only quaint, is astonishingly like that given by modern astronomers, who tell us that all the visible stars belong to a single galaxy, and revolve slowly around what might be described as a fiery center—packed as it is, from our distant perspective, with the billions of stars of the Milky Way.

Whence, Pythagoras's amazing knowledge? Surely, no theory so all-embracing could have sprung out of the common knowledge of his times. It must be attributed, first, to the expansiveness of his own consciousness.

In this Twentieth Century a great deal has been written, albeit somewhat superficially, on the importance of self-knowledge, and of acting in keeping with that knowledge. Nora, in Ibsen's play *The Doll House,* was one of the first examples of this doctrine. So also was Kate, the protagonist in J. M. Barrie's *The Twelve Pound Look*. Both women chose to live their lives self-reliantly, rather than continue in bondage to their boorish and condescending husbands. In more recent years, the quantity of this sort of literature has grown apace, along with hundreds of classes and seminars offering techniques of self-fulfillment.

It would be no great stretch further to bring this emphasis into the high schools and universities. The process is, in fact, already underway.

The question still remains to be asked: How to know oneself as one *really* is?

Is it enough to follow the lead of Nora and Kate?—to stand up to the world and cry, "From today on I'm going to be my own boss"? More than self-assertion is called for, if self-knowledge is to be achieved.

One of the best exponents of the "personal fulfillment" philosophy in our times was the existentialist Jean Paul Sartre. Sartre claimed that it is people's self-generated desires that define them as they really are. He insisted that if we will but rid ourselves of the expectations other people hold of us, and be true to our own nature, we will become genuine human beings at last. And if the final outcome of this supposedly purifying process should make us social outcasts, why, so be it. In remaining stalwartly true to ourselves, we will—by Sartre's definition—deserve to be called saints.

Sartre even wrote a book titled *Saint Genet,* about a man who, faithful to these "principles," dared both to be and to boast about being a thief and a male prostitute.

The writings of Sartre have been avidly studied, as though they were actually important to the quest for fulfillment. Sartre was, however, a nihilist. He accepted no established human norms. And he was not joking. Nor has his influence on modern society been a joke. One sees the effect of his philosophy on the behavior of countless young people today—many of them barely pubescent—who self-assertively proclaim that life is meaningless and who behave, accordingly, with egocentric abandon.

One wonders: Why have these nihilistic teachings been given so solemn a hearing in the classrooms, especially when there exists a vast body of time-tested teachings on the subject of meaningful self-fulfillment? Yet this material is virtually ignored.

Sartre's grotesque distortion of man's eternal quest will eventually, I believe, prove the sterility of his own case. For his examples of "fulfilled" human beings make it clear with repetitive monotony to the discerning mind how vast is the distance between ego-affirmation and Self-realization. There is a radical difference between the ego and the deeper self, the experience of which is an awakening, a goal implied in the saying "Know thyself."

Greatness has always been associated with an expansion of consciousness. And an expansion of consciousness has always, in the long history of civilization, been associated with an expansion of such feelings as sympathy, empathy, and love. Far from setting oneself apart from, or even against, other human beings, self-expansion naturally includes a concern for the well-being of all. How different, this, from the teaching of Sartre, which he stated in these words: "To be conscious of another is to be conscious of what one is not."

Consider, therefore, the great teachers of mankind—Buddha, Krishna, and Moses, for example, and of course, best known in the West, Jesus Christ. Their teachings receive hardly a passing nod in the modern classroom. Why this disdain? Is it merely because those men of wisdom are now considered "old hat"? Can anyone really expect the philosophy of Sartre to replace wisdom that has been cultivated with hard labor by spiritual geniuses through the ages? What can this fascination with that dour philosopher, and with others of his genre, be but a fad, merely?

A likely explanation for the attention presently being given to this and to similarly faddish philosophies is that they offer no call to serious action. They suit the intellectual's disdain for personal commitment, and flatter his preference for clever theories over demonstrable truths. The intellectual's favorite weapon is not honest reasoning, but mockery. But mockery is a coward's weapon. It is a saber rattled within the seemingly safe fortress of untested theory. The fortress itself, however, is merely a stage set, painted to look real, but the merest spark of clear reasoning may send it crashing down in flames. Jesus and countless other great men and women through the ages began and ended their message with warnings against remaining satisfied with mere theory, and with a call to action—to direct, personal experience of the truths they proclaimed. To the intellectual—or perhaps I should call him the *pseudo*-intellectual, since he uses intellectuality without discrimination—any moral principle that can be tested by actual experience seems drab and uninteresting. Far more appealing to him are theories that only he, and perhaps a few other precious souls like him, can understand.

The common explanation, of course, for not including spiritual teachings in the classroom is that formal education is concerned with imparting demonstrable facts, and not with dogmatizing students in unproven sectarian claims. I grant you, it is a bit much to hear people describe universal truths as the *possession* of any particular religion: to hear humility, for instance, described as "Christian" humility, as though Christian humility were different in some fundamental respect from Buddhist humility, or Hindu humility. Strip the veneer of religion away from the quality of humility, however, and you find a human characteristic that can be tested for its value to us all in our search for personal fulfillment. Why leave it buried in the Bible simply because Jesus spoke well of it?

Qualities such as humility are by no means untested sectarian dogmas. It doesn't take much experience of life to see that pride does in fact "go before a fall," as the wisdom of the ages has always told us; and that genuine humility "works"—that is to say, it attracts what people really want in life: success, support from others, and an ability to ride the waves of difficulty. Humility, like countless other virtues, is a practical concept. Why not teach it that way in the classroom?

There are numerous other teachings, born of practical human experience, that are the discoveries of people who showed by their own lives that they had found keys to unlock the door to human happiness. Their discoveries have nothing to do with religious sectarianism. Why exclude them from the teaching we give our young?

Great men and women, whether scientists or artists or leaders of any kind, are great in some way, at least, *as human beings.* Were this not so, they would never be able to manifest what it took to produce their great works. Is it enough, then, merely to study their *works?* Children need to be offered also a study of what makes people great as human beings. In this way, the children may be inspired toward greatness themselves. Is this not self-evidently better than giving them what is, essentially, the philosophical encouragement to become thieves and murderers? For that is what it amounts to when we tell them, with Sartre, that all values are relative, and that truth is anything you yourself want it to be.

Chapter 6

Punishment and Reward

"Spare the rod and spoil the child." This saying was popular, or at least widely quoted, even in more or less recent times. It is unacceptable today, and I think with good cause. To *force* a child to be good is to awaken in him a resentment that will probably find full expression once he attains the "dignity" of adulthood.

Children *can* be spoiled. To spoil a child is to raise him in the belief that he can always get his own way, perhaps by temper tantrums, perhaps by wheedling and flattery, perhaps by playing one adult against another. (Children can be master manipulators!) It is necessary for the child to grow up with the awareness that the world is not there to do just what *he* wants.

Nevertheless, liberal use of the "rod" can also spoil the most beautiful aspect of a child's nature: the quality of trust. To my mind, this kind of spoiling is even worse than giving a child free rein to indulge his every whim. For although the world shows him soon enough its massive indifference to his whims, without trust in life the child will grow up to be cynical. People who trust, and who trust in the power of love, can cope far better with life's setbacks than those who have been schooled by punishment.

Behaviorists understand punishment and reward as a way of human conditioning. To employ this method without compassion and wisdom, however, is to manipulate others and, as the behaviorist B.F. Skinner noted approvingly in his book, *Walden II,* to "play

God." We have no right, as human beings, to control the lives of others, even if it is our duty to teach children right behavior. The punishment-reward method of training children is, rightly I think, offensive to the modern mentality, and is opposed by most modern methods of education.

Still, it is a fact of Nature that punishment and reward *is* the system by which all creatures learn. The important thing is as much as possible to allow Nature herself to do the teaching.

And so she does, quite effectively. Things are so arranged in the great scheme of things that we soon learn the lessons we need for our own survival and well being . If we touch a hot stove, for example, we burn our fingers. It shouldn't require more than one such lesson for us to learn that the human skin was not made to have intense heat inflicted on it.

On countless other levels of our lives we learn that, by living in accordance with natural law, we prosper; but by flouting that law, we suffer.

The important point is that natural law is centered in every molecule, in every atom. It is a radiation, an expansion, outward from that center, and not an imposition from without. The lesson it teaches us is that that same natural center exists everywhere, and must be respected even as we respect our own center within ourselves. To paraphrase the words of Paramhansa Yogananda, universal law is "center everywhere, circumference nowhere." Life teaches us to be sensitive to other realities than our own, including other people's realities. In this way, life brings us, bit by bit, to the ultimate refinement of maturity.

Adults should be sensitive to a child's need for awareness of these broader realities. To command the child, "Don't you dare touch that stove!" is to offend against the natural order of things. Maturity comes not by commandment, but by gradual recognition. Thus, it would be wiser to cooperate with, and not to short-circuit, this process.

Here, then, enters the necessity for wise guidance. For every child, as well as every situation, is in some way unique. Some situations call for a more urgent response than others. Certainly, you wouldn't let your child burn his hand on a hot stove. If he approaches it, you will instinctively cry out to him, "Don't touch that!" Not to explain to him afterward, however, why you warned him so urgently might be to leave him baffled, even confused. Perhaps, the next time he gets the opportunity, and finds himself alone in the kitchen, he may hesitantly go to the stove and touch it. If it is still hot, it will burn him. And perhaps it is necessary that he have this experience. At least, this time, he will do so tentatively, only. But best of all is for him to be by nature reasonable, and willing to heed your rea-soned explanation as to why hot stoves should not be touched.

This is a simplistic example. Life gives us many more difficult lessons to learn: why it isn't good to hurt others; why it is good to share with them; why anger is so often self-defeating as a means of getting one's own way; why material gain is, in itself, not satisfying. We want to spare others the need to learn every lesson through pain, but a wise parent or teacher knows that there are lessons, even painful ones, that can be learned only by actual experience.

"Spare the rod and spoil the child." We have simply to accept that Life itself applies this truth impartially to everyone, whether children or adults. And we have to accept also that if this weren't life's law, we would never attain true maturity. We would in effect become spoiled because ignorant of broader realities than those of our own petty egos and our own selfish desires.

A successful businessman was once asked the secret of his success. He replied, "I allowed those under me to make mistakes, and to learn by them." How many businessmen, by contrast, will even dismiss a subordinate for making a mistake. Ruthless leaders are notoriously intolerant of error in those serving under them. The consequence is that those people, fearful of stumbling, become stiffly unnatural in everything they do and lose altogether any tendency they may have had to be creative.

Education should be a means of encouraging, not of forcing, the development of wisdom. It should work *with* Nature in its inherent system of punishment and reward, and not protect children from the consequences of all their mistakes. At the same time, it should try to ease them into the discovery of these consequences in such a way that they don't lose heart, but come to realize that such, simply, are life's realities.

One excellent way of cooperating with Nature is to draw their attention to what they themselves have experienced as a result of their actions and attitudes. There is no harm even in setting up situations that will help them to learn these truths for themselves. Always, however, the lessons should be directed toward encouraging recognition *from within,* and not a didactic lesson that leaves them with the impression that you have said, in effect, "See? I told you so!" The child must be left with the thought, "I learned this lesson all by myself."

Why should we be honest, and not dishonest? truthful, and not untruthful? self-controlled, and not self-abandoned? concentrated in our thinking, and not scattered? kind, and not callous? cooperative, and not over-competitive? *Why?* Not because anyone holds out these expectations of us, but simply because the positive side of each of these equations gives us, in the end, what we really want from life. It isn't scripture, or the government, or society, or anyone's personal convenience that dictates our need to live rightly. Natural law itself—the law of our own being—is so set up that only by harmonizing ourselves with it can we, in the long run, find our real needs served—even, if you like, our selfish needs. But refusal to harmonize ourselves with that law invariably proves disappointing *to us* in the end.

That, of course, is what makes wrong action wrong in the first place: It is culpable, not before God, nor before the law of the land, nor before our fellow human beings, but before the inner court of our own self-awareness.

Chapter 7

To What End?

A woman of my acquaintance one day, in an effort to break her two-year-old child of certain infantile habits, said to him, "Come on now, you're not a baby any longer."

The toddler looked up at her with a happy smile and replied, "But I *like* being a baby!"

Another friend of mine was once asked by her five-year-old daughter, "Mommy, what do you think about during the day?"

"Well," the mother replied, "I think about you children, about Daddy, about our friends."

"I don't," rejoined the little girl, quite seriously. "I think about *me*." She paused a bit, then continued thoughtfully, "Why do little children think about themselves?"

Interesting conversations, both of them.

We assume that children have a *desire* to grow up. But even adults are prone to resist change. How much more so, then, babies, secure in the loving embrace of their mothers; or little children, more interested in themselves than in the world—what to speak of the vast universe?—around them.

And yet, even at such a young age my friend's little daughter was able also to universalize her self-preoccupation, to expand her identity to include other children. She displayed an inclination that is present in everyone, including children, not only to cling to what they already know, but also to enlarge their horizons, if only gradually and by small increments.

Indeed, expansion is instinctive to life itself. The important thing to understand, especially where children are concerned, is that they need to be *invited* to grow toward maturity. The ever-expanding vision of reality that will be theirs during the growing-up process must be offered to them sensitively. Otherwise, instead of awakening their interest, it may repel them.

Even adults may feel themselves threatened by challenges that are too far beyond their present horizons. I well remember something I observed personally in this connection.

Of the diverse activities that engage a person during his lifetime, my own have happened to include the founding of a community. This village, in fact, during some thirty years of struggles and challenges, has managed to grow and even to flourish. But when it was new it manifested—as often happens with projects at their outset—few of the outward signs of success.

Sometimes, in those days, I would share with others my dreams for the community's future. My intention was to inspire, but, to my astonishment, these dreams for the future proved more threatening, for many, than inspiring. From that experience I learned that people need to advance one step at a time instead of making a giant mental leap into the future. In our case it was gradually only, as our members' familiarity with the experiment developed over the years, that they found themselves accepting the developments I'd described, and much greater developments, which indeed they embraced quite naturally and happily.

Some of the principles of right behavior may at first seem contrary to common sense. It seems like simple common sense, for example, to cater to our own needs even at the cost of the needs of others. Yet mature people have always endorsed unselfishness as more deeply self-fulfilling. If such a teaching, however, defies common sense in many adults, how can we expect children to embrace it easily? One even wonders whether the little ones don't sometimes feel themselves lost in a wilderness of adult values.

A cousin of mine, as a child, was always getting into scrapes. He was physically very strong, and therefore always came out the victor. One afternoon he returned home with a torn shirt and a few bruises. His mother admonished him, "Don't you know, dear, that when another boy hits you, you shouldn't hit him back?"

"Oh, but Mother," the boy replied self-righteously, "I *never* hit back. I *always* hit first!"

It isn't easy to teach such a child principles that we may value. Their experience of life, so far, falls far short of our own. How can we encourage them to include others' realities in their own? Precepts that can be taught to an adult may be difficult even to explain to a child. In fact, let's face it, even adults don't always take to them easily. ("So he'll starve if I take his job away from him. What of it? It's a jungle out there—survival of the fittest and all that. I gotta think about *me*.")

The task of education is to attract children toward the ideals of maturity—that is, toward including others' realities in their own. A child has a natural need to feel secure within boundaries already known to him. Fortunately for his own development, he also feels an inherent need to expand those boundaries, even though gradually, as he senses in himself the capability to push them outward.

Many of the fantasies of childhood, for example, though they may appear foolish in the eyes of literal-minded adults, are important to children. If a child believes in Santa Claus, for instance, don't disillusion him. Take him step by step, and not in one sudden leap, toward an understanding of things as they really are. If he is guided sensitively, he will keep the priceless gift of imagination, without which no great achievements in life are remotely possible.

Again, a child needs to know what his limits are; he is unhappy if he receives no guideline at all. To be told, "No, you may *not* cross the street unattended," may invoke in him an uncomprehending disagreement, but it is a necessary guideline nevertheless, and the very firmness of the limits it imposes will give him a sense of security.

The child must be allowed to expand his understanding at his own pace. He should be encouraged, but never forced, in this direction by his adult mentors.

It would help, however, to find one, all-encompassing explanation for the bewildering number of precepts he needs to learn as he grows up, *one single* principle that he will recognize as a constant.

He may not quickly understand the need, for example, to include others' realities in his own. He may not easily perceive the benefits to himself of being generous to others. He may find himself merely bewildered by the—again, to him—incredible suggestion that, when hit, he shouldn't hit back. And in teaching him each of these precepts, it may be difficult to get him to memorize them, presented as each one might be, separately and without any relation to other precepts.

What is needed is some simple "Unified Field Theory" (for lack of a better term) applied to human behavior; one that will avoid that common, but minimally effective, explanation, "If you don't do as I say, you'll get a walloping!"

And in fact there is such an explanation. It is one that can serve well for all the stages of a child's journey toward true maturity, and is equally relevant for adults.

For, regardless of any other motivation, there is in all striving *one over-riding consideration.* Though true equally for adults and children, it is easier to discern, usually, in the life of a child. For the child's motivations are less easily hidden by other considerations: "What will the neighbors think? Will devoting energy to my family damage me in my career? Will smiling at my customers, regardless how I feel inside, boost my income?" The child's motivations are seldom so complex.

What people *really* want, at the heart of everything they do, is quite simple: They want to avoid the experience of pain, and to exchange it for the experience of happiness. This simple thought was, to the best of my knowledge, expressed first by the great Indian sage, Paramhansa Yogananda. We could therefore name it (though he himself never did so) "Yogananda's Law of Basic Motivation." Put in the simplest terms, this is the Law: *The twofold goal of all human striving is the avoidance of pain, and the fulfillment of happiness.*

Why, for example, does a grown-up seek employment? First, because he wants to escape the pain of hunger and financial insecurity; second, because he wants to find happiness—whether happiness in the work itself, or happiness through the things he expects to be able to afford once he has a steady income.

Why do people climb mountains? Is it only "to get to the top" (or, like Hillary, "because it's there")? Why would anyone *want* to get to the top of a mountain? Quite simply, because the climber has it in his mind that at the top lies, for him, some kind of fulfillment—in other words, happiness.

And why do people resort to collecting—as a recent bulk mailing invited me to do—"artistic replicas" in silver of emblems on the hoods of automobiles in the early nineteen-twenties? All, one assumes, to escape what must, for some, be the intolerable agony of not owning such a collection, and, on the positive side, for the sheer ecstasy of possessing one.

It depends simply on what desires you've cultivated in your heart. *"Le monde,"* as the French say, *"où l'on s'amuse."*

Within the vast panorama of human desires, however, there may be seen certain types of behavior that receive universal approval or disapproval. Whether climbing mountains or collecting emblems is viewed favorably or unfavorably depends entirely on the individual's point of view. It has been well said that there is no accounting for taste. When it comes to traits of character, however, mere taste is not the point. Kindness vs. cruelty, generosity vs. selfishness, calmness vs. nervousness, cheerfulness and similar positive attitudes vs. negativity and moodiness, sharing the credit vs. claiming all the credit for oneself: There lies at some level in every human being, even the most egocentric, a recognition at least that a choice is involved in each of these cases, and that this choice can be crucial in a person's life.

The choice is in fact more crucial than most people realize. Whatever the trait under discussion, the issues concerned can be explained with perfect clarity in these simple, basic terms: *By right behavior, a person (a child, in this case) will avoid pain to himself; even more important, he will increase his own measure of happiness.*

Chapter 8

Humanizing the Process

Sir Roy Redgrave, former Commander of the British armed forces in the Far East, and a childhood friend of mine, once remarked to me, "The character of every regiment is determined by its leadership."

The same is true of businesses, of monasteries, and of any activity where groups of people are involved. The spirit of the leader, or leaders, determines both the character and the spirit of the group. Hence, the importance of developing leadership in those children who show a talent for it.

Hence also the importance, in schools, of developing effective teachers. For if children are to be taught according to this new system called "Education for Life," it is imperative that the teachers be trained first in the system, lest old and habitual methods of teaching reassert themselves later.

To teach these principles, special studies will need to be developed. Special teacher training will be necessary.

There is much also, however, that might be done with conventional subjects to impart the basic principles of Education for Life. The important thing would be to humanize the process as much as possible, that it be made relevant to the actual needs and interests of the students.

Here are a few suggestions for how this humanizing might be achieved—suggestions which I hope will, in turn, help spark other creative ideas in teachers' minds.

Humanizing History

History teachers might make it a point not to teach history only as a series of events long past, but as a guideline for the students' own present and future life. Consider the Battle of Agincourt as an example.

In 1415 A.D., King Henry V of England, against seemingly impossible odds, vanquished the flower of French chivalry by introducing a new method of warfare. His way was to rely on his foot soldiers, especially on those who wielded the English longbow. The French knights came unprepared for this kind of battle, and lost heavily. From then on, victory no longer depended on knights in armor. Agincourt was a victory not only for the English, but for the inspired use of common sense.

Another battle, similar in the resourcefulness of the weaker party, was fought during the middle ages by Swiss peasants against their aristocratic overlords. The peasants had for weapons only their scythes and pitchforks. The noblemen rode horses and were heavily armed and armored.

What the peasants did was flood the battlefield on the eve of battle with water from a nearby river. It was the dead of winter, and the water froze overnight. When the oppressors sallied forth on the following morning, the horses slipped and fell all over the ice. The peasants came to battle shod for walking on ice, and dispatched the lot of them with ease.

What practical lessons might a child learn from these and other similar examples in history? Well, for one thing, he could be taught that solutions to problems often depend on being solution-oriented, rather than problem-oriented; that opposite cases—in other words, history's outstanding failures—often resulted when people brooded on the hopelessness of their situation, instead of casting about expectantly for a way out of it.

Children might also learn that creative initiative can accomplish far more than brute force; and determined energy, far more than complacent power.

Again, they might learn that traditional ways of doing things are not always the best; that a fresh and better approach usually requires pulling back mentally a little bit, and casting about for a better way.

History is full of examples that can be similarly turned to useful advantage. And wouldn't it be vastly more enjoyable to learn the story of the past, and for that matter to teach it, in its relevance to actual needs of the present? What matter, if a few minor dates, events, and individuals in history receive less mention, or even none, for lack of the time usually devoted to them? One must be selective in any case regarding what one teaches. Why not be selective, then, with an eye also to the students' actual needs?

Humanizing the Instruction of Languages

An important subject, nowadays especially, is foreign languages.

It would be helpful, at the outset, to offer as a new academic course an overview of general linguistic trends. Such a course could include a study of how languages evolve; of basic differences between one language and another; of the source of words; and of how the use of words actually helps to direct the way we think.

Take, for example, the Romance, or Latin-based, languages. These, unlike English, assign a gender to every noun. When you start a sentence in French, Spanish, or Italian, you must already be committed to whatever nouns you plan to use in the sentence. Only by knowing in advance whether those nouns are masculine or feminine can you know what modifying articles, adjectives, and adverbs to start out with.

When speaking those languages, one is obliged to be conscious not only of concepts, but of the specific words one intends to use to express those concepts. Such uncompromisingly logical speech forces itself, with its advantages but also disadvantages, on the very way people in those countries view life.

English, by contrast, has been described as an intuitive language. You can "switch horses" in the midstream of an English sentence, selecting at a moment's notice, perhaps, some new word that you hadn't thought to use at first, but that you now see will suit your purpose better.

The ultimate purpose of this sort of study is that it makes the student more flexible mentally, more aware of other ways of thinking and looking at things than those to which he has been raised. Respect for another person's mental processes is part of what it means to be mature—to be aware of, and thus to relate to, that person's realities, and not only to one's own. Lest this analysis strike the reader as a value judgment in favor of English and against French and other languages, I should add that maturity is too complex an issue to be determined by anything so simplistic as the outer garments of a language.

The point of the "Education for Life" system, however, is not only to draw morals from what one teaches. Too much moralizing, indeed, can become dreary, even if the goal of it all is to guide the student toward deeper understanding. But one of the greatest lessons that life teaches is how to *enjoy* what we do— and, in the classroom, how to enjoy whatever one teaches, or learns.

In this respect, conventional pedagogy, rooted as it is in the transmission of a fixed body of knowledge, tends toward sterility. The learning process ought to be rooted in life itself, and therefore—for the teacher quite as much as for the student—a thing fresh and wonderful every day. Any teacher who really *enjoys* what he teaches, and who can spark a kindred enjoyment in his students, has already mastered one of the central points in the Education for Life system.

If conventional teaching suggests few creative insights to the average student's mind, it is because facts by themselves are static. Excessive devotion to committing facts to memory actively discourages dynamic creative thought. Teachers themselves who teach by this method easily sink into a rut of teaching from habit, out of the depths of which they may view only with resentment any attempt to dislodge them.

The very examples teachers often use in their instruction offer little challenge to the imagination. We were discussing the teaching of languages. A delightfully stuffy book of guidelines that I was once shown for the English-speaking tourist in Germany included this helpful sentence: "Stop, barber, you have put the brush in my mouth!" Much can be done, however, to inspire students to identify themselves with the mental outlook of an Italian, for example, when learning Italian; with that of a Frenchman, when learning French, and so on. The art of learning languages is to a great extent a matter of "tuning in" to the general consciousness of the people who speak it.

Every language has a peculiar "melody," or lilt. This melody is, in my opinion, as important in its own way as the words and grammar of the language, for it contains its inner "feeling," without which no language is living, and from which the words themselves evolve. Without that inner "feeling" of a language, mere words and grammar are like Esperanto—interesting, but essentially an abstraction. You can't master a language if you can't emerge from the consciousness and attitudes of an American (or whatever your own nationality is). One hears the advice, "Learn to *think* in the language you are studying." Actually, much more is involved. *Be* a Frenchman, in attitude, if you want to learn French. *Be* a German, or an Italian. There would be no harm in even getting students to dress the part, to enter the role with their gestures, and above all to abandon their natural shyness at moving their lips, tongues, and faces in unaccustomed, but necessary, ways to speak like a native. The children can, moreover, have great fun with this practice. (I'll never forget the challenge I faced with the broad "A" in Italian. In my efforts to master this language, getting that "A" right seemed quite like crossing the Rubicon!)

I've mentioned the "melody" of a language. Rhythm, too, is important. Every language has certain rhythms that are peculiar to itself. Melody and rhythm are intrinsic to music, which is another mode of communication entirely from the spoken word. Without them, much meaning would never be conveyed. And without them, I dare say, no one would ever learn a language perfectly, or even very well.

The purely mental approach to learning is shown at its greatest disadvantage, perhaps, in the study of languages. Most of us have also been through the dry declensions of nouns, the "amo-amas-amatting" of Latin verbs, the presentation of even living languages as though they were already dead and mummified. I once saw a cartoon in The New Yorker magazine: a sign in a Paris shop that read, "College French spoken here."

In my own experience, I recall getting low marks in a course in French even though, having spent a year and a half as a boy in French Switzerland, I spoke the language better than my teacher (or so he told me). But I'd learned French by speaking it. I couldn't relate this living language that I knew to the sterile lists we'd been given to memorize in the classroom.

Why not include in the study of languages a study also of the people who speak them—their history, their national traits, their heroes? Why not study language, in other words, *from its inner heart?*

If, for example, the subject is Italian, it will help enormously to identify, from your own heart, with the Italian people, and not to look upon them as "those crazy people with this weird tendency to finish every word with an *a*." That is what Italians and their noble language are likely to remain for the student, if all he learns in the classroom is verb forms dangled at him in mid-air, and tangled in stilted sentences.

From the standpoint of the Education for Life system, there is much to be gained from learning to approach *any* new subject as it were *from within*—from its core, rather than from its periphery. And one way to accomplish this feat is for the student to be involved totally in whatever subject he or she is given to study.

And what matter if, in the process, traditional teaching lines have to be crossed? For a language teacher to teach a little of Italy's history along with its language may constitute a minor incursion into the history teacher's domain, but where is the harm in getting the student to see the same history from a broader perspective?

Indeed, it is partly in the rigid compartmentalizing of subjects that formal education loses so much of its potential relevance. Compartmentalized knowledge somewhat resembles an approach to the study of the human body by examining the head alone, then the lungs alone, then the intestines alone, and so forth, while ignoring the living interrelationship of the different parts to one another. Medical education, in fact, errs in just this respect.

I have often played with an idea that, unfortunately, I don't see as workable very soon in the schools, but it is worth including here for future students of this subject: to have every study for a certain period of time revolve around an over-all subject that is relevant to all of them.

I first got this idea from a two-week study I did in the fine points of English grammar. It was the sort of study that might easily have taken a year to complete in a standard curriculum. Such a long time frame, and the necessity for hopping back and forth between this subject and four or five others, doing homework daily in all six fields, would have left me a comparative outsider to all of them, including the subject of English grammar. I'm sure I would not have learned grammar nearly so well in a year as I was able to in two weeks of steady concentration on the subject.

How good it would be, I thought, if this kind of concentration could be devoted to every subject studied. Most young people are too mentally restless to focus on only one subject at a time, but one way to make such concentration possible would be to arrange the other subjects around a single focus, so that all of them conspired to help the student really to enter into what he was studying.

An idea, only. But I must admit, I like it.

Humanizing Mathematics

In the study of mathematics, too, considerable interest in the subject might be sparked by including in the course a general history of mathematics. Interesting, too, would be a study of the lives of great mathematicians, and perhaps of the challenges they faced in getting their work accepted.

Great mathematicians often have a sense of the sheer poetry of numbers—a sense that is seldom hinted at, and perhaps not even imagined, by most teachers of mathematics courses.

There is Pythagoras's application of mathematics to the study of music: a fascinating subject, but one that is rarely even mentioned in the classroom.

Of great and practical interest to students of algebra would be a study of the importance of symbolic logic in everyday life—of making definitions serve in place of complex realities as a means of simplifying one's thoughts about them. The advantages, and also the disadvantages, of symbolic thinking make a fascinating and important study.

For we engage in it all the time, consciously or unconsciously, on every level of our lives. There is, for example, symbolic emotional thinking, where a person will say one thing but mean quite another and expect to be understood. There is the symbolism of poetry, with its use of rain, for instance, to imply sorrow, or spring flowers to suggest new beginnings. And there is the importance of learning to distinguish between symbolic and literal thought—the importance, in other words, of learning not to confuse definition with reality.

Children in the lower grades, on the other hand, could have emphasized to them, when faced with arithmetic's immutable rules, the importance of accepting and adapting to things *as they are*. Two plus two always makes four; it is not a matter of whim. The children may have become used to getting their own way in certain matters, but here is an example, selected from countless realities in life, of something that no amount of wishing will be able to change.

There is even something that might be taught—a point, incidentally, of considerable interest: that different types of human activity require different directions of energy. Language and music, for example, require a greater focus of energy in the heart: a "feeling" energy. Mathematics and logic, on the other hand, are more mental; they are easier to grasp when the mind is focused, as the yogis of India suggest, at the seat of concentration in the body, midway between the eyebrows.

The mastery of any subject requires that one identify himself with the particular state of consciousness appropriate to that subject. To learn mathematics, one must try to *think* like a mathematician. To learn French, one must try to think like a Frenchman. To learn cooking, one must think like a cook. To learn skiing, one must assume the attitude of a good skier.

The Importance of Fantasy

For young children especially, the importance of fantasy should not be overlooked. History, for example, might be taught as though seen through the eyes of a child traveling back in a time machine to centuries long past, and relating what he sees to their own lives today.

Geography, again, might be taught as seen through the eyes of a boy and girl traveling to distant places, and experiencing exotic sights in terms of their own immediate realities.

In every field, even the most prosaic, there are endless opportunities for creative application of Education for Life principles to make the subjects more immediately human, and less abstract and statistical.

Chapter 9

The Importance, to Understanding, of Experience

Much can be done in the teaching of conventional subjects to educate children in the art of living. In order seriously to offer them an Education for Life, however, special training in this art of teaching needs to be offered as well, both in special classes and outside the classroom.

An intellectual understanding of how to live is never sufficient. Even in so intellectual a subject as algebra, John Saxon, a teacher famous for the efficacy of his methods, has demonstrated the importance of grounding students in constant practice.

Saxon has convinced many teachers of the appeal of humor, moreover, and of offering down-to-earth, human situations when presenting a problem. In his book, *Algebra I,* he wrote: "At the Mardi Gras ball, the guests roistered and rollicked until the wee hours. If the ratio of roisterers to rollickers was 7 to 5 and 1080 were in attendance, how many were rollickers?" Students generally find this sort of problem much more fun to consider than, let us say, the ratio of trucks to wheelbarrows filled with cement. Math problems are commonly stated with no thought at all to giving the students a good time. It is almost like the notorious "Protestant ethic": "If you enjoy it, it can't be good for you."

If in conventional studies there is a need for experience in the sense of repeated practice, and not only for intellectual explanation—a point hotly contested, incidentally, by the majority of Saxon's peers in the school system—how self-evidently is it true for the living values that are the focus of the present book.

Well, on second thought, perhaps it is too sanguine to call it self-evident. For we live today in a society that holds practically as a dogma the notion that to define a thing is to understand it. All teaching, virtually, is of the blackboard, variety: "Spell it out, and you'll understand it."

Many a psychiatrist considers it the limit of his duty to get a patient to "see" the point he is making. "Yes, Doc, it's true, I have a low self-image." Very well; and then? Even at this point, how much has really been achieved?

I have known many highly intelligent people who pride themselves on the range and subtlety of their self-understanding, but who never take the first step toward actual self-betterment. It is as though, by mental acceptance of the need for making a change, they somehow imagined that the change had already occurred!

The more intelligent a person, it often seems, the more difficult it is for him to make a serious commitment to positive action.

Of course, I am not referring to intelligence *per se.* The greatest deeds in any field of endeavor are always performed by people of exceptional intelligence. My reference, rather, is to those whose intelligence is, in a manner of speaking, ingrown; whose intellectuality tends to isolate them from objective reality, or to leave them satisfied with merely reading or thinking about reality. Such intellection only paralyzes the will.

This, indeed, as I have already said, is a basic weakness of our modern educational system. The very people who are the most involved in the system—the teachers and professors—are those, usually, who are the most resistant to change of any kind. Their intellectual bias is toward theories, and toward a corresponding lack of practical commitment to anything.

Much can be accomplished in the way of giving children an Education for Life even while teaching standard classroom subjects. Special classes in the art of living need to be taught also, however, classes filled with narrative examples, practical illustrations, and useful techniques that the children themselves can practice in the classroom and at home.

There need to be classes in self-expression; in understanding oneself and others; in the benefits of cooperation with others; in the true meaning of success; in how to succeed at anything; in how to have a positive influence on others; in joyful self-discipline; in the importance of right, positive attitudes; in the art of concentration; in developing memory; in general problem-solving; in secrets of achieving true happiness. The list given here is by no means exhaustive; it is intended to suggest a direction that, if pursued, will open up ever-fresh possibilities. Suffice it to say that the classes should as much as possible be *experiential,* not didactic.

Outside the classroom, time should be set apart for a more spontaneous, more individualized type of education. In this respect it is a pity that most education is only a daytime affair. Far more can be accomplished with students who live full time at the school during the school months.

Paramhansa Yogananda, the noted spiritual leader and teacher, when directing the boys' boarding school he'd founded at Ranchi, India, discovered that two of his students were bitter enemies. He tried counseling, but his attempt at advice proved a failure; they lacked the motivation to "bury the hatchet."

He then had them share the same bed. After that, it was either constant warfare or grudging peace. After struggling for some time with the issue, they decided on peace. Gradually, indeed, they became friends.

After some weeks, Yogananda decided to bring the lesson home to them on an even deeper level. Tiptoeing silently to the head of their bed as they slept, he reached down cautiously and rapped one of them on the forehead, immediately withdrawing his arm.

The boy rose up wrathfully and accused his bed-mate of breaking the peace.

"I didn't hit you, I swear it!" cried the other, wide-eyed with surprise.

Both settled back to sleep. After a few minutes, when they were sleeping soundly again, Yogananda rapped the other boy on the forehead.

"I told you I didn't do it!" cried the second boy angrily. They were on the point of blows when, looking up, they beheld their school principal smiling down at them.

"Oh," they exclaimed in amazement. *"You!"*

This shared experience, and the humorous light that it cast on their previous enmity, cemented their friendship from that time onward.

I grant you, this sort of teaching demands both the right occasion and the right teacher. The limitations imposed by daytime education, however, make such in-depth training all the more difficult. And the difficulty of finding wise teachers makes teacher-training, and a greater appreciation on the part of society for the role of teachers, imperative.

Meanwhile, what can be accomplished with things as they now stand?

It is difficult, even in the most ordinary situations, to avoid artificiality when seeking to convey direct experience to a child. The very act of saying, "Now we're going to experience how and why it is good to forgive others," not only creates a false situation, but also encourages a merely superficial response.

Obviously, then, teachers need to be aware of, and quickly responsive to, situations as they actually arise in the lives of their students. The test of a teacher's wisdom will lie in his ability to recognize a problem, and to respond to it sensitively and appropriately.

For instance, were a teacher to leap enthusiastically at every opportunity to instruct his students in the art of living the moment any such opportunity presents itself, he might well develop in them, gradually, a resentment toward all instruction in human values.

I knew a teacher who suffered from this excess of zeal. A girl in his class had an accident on her bicycle one day. She was lying, curled up and weeping, in the school driveway, when the teacher crouched down beside her.

"Now, Nancy," he demanded insistently, "analyze your thoughts. *Why* did you have this accident? Be honest with yourself. You're trying to escape something, aren't you? Can't you see that you've *attracted* this experience?"

Poor child! All she needed just then was a little comfort and sympathy. And if the teacher was correct in believing that her need arose from some deep self-deception, what of it? People deceive themselves constantly and in countless ways. To reproach her on such an obvious issue, when she was at her most vulnerable, displayed an insufferable sense of superiority and belief in his own infallibility.

Love a child when he weeps, and he may be the more ready to listen to reason after he's calmed down. And maybe it isn't really reasoning that he needs anyway.

It is difficult enough to deal wisely with living situations. It is far more difficult to create them artificially, for the purposes of instruction.

Much, however, can be accomplished by a sort of deliberate artificiality, in the form of fantasy: stories acted out; little dramatic pieces; story-reading that involves the children's response and verbal participation.

In this respect, an excellent lesson can be taken from the children themselves. For what is the universal game played by children everywhere, regardless of culture or nationality? *Let's pretend:*

"You be the dragon, Johnny. Jeannie, you be the princess. And I'll be the prince who comes to the castle and saves her, riding on a white horse and holding a shiny sword."

Or:

"Here is the dragon. He was once a soldier who wanted to protect his princess. One day, he fought off the attack of an evil wizard who wanted to carry the princess off to his dungeon. The wizard then cursed him to become a dragon, and to become as mean and violent as dragons usually are.

"Now that same dragon won't let anyone near his princess, and is doomed by the curse to lay the countryside to waste for miles around with his fiery breath. No knight can destroy him, no matter how sharp or shiny his sword.

"If anyone can *forgive* him, however—deeply, from his heart—his forgiveness will break the evil spell cast by the wizard. By forgiveness, the dragon will be turned back into a good and loyal soldier. And the brave knight who saved him will marry the princess."

The children might also have fun fantasizing the dragon's rejection of any forgiveness that didn't proceed from deep enough feeling in the heart.

An important point to be realized, when helping children to achieve fresh insight into the problems they encounter in daily life, is that the intellectual understanding of a problem is not only insufficient, but often is not helpful at all. What *is* important is that they find themselves moving happily in a new direction, and not that they themselves understand all the reasons for the direction.

I am reminded here of a story from the life of St. Francis of Assisi. St. Francis and a small group of his friars minor were walking one day along a country road, singing joyfully of God's love. At a turn in the road, a stranger appeared and threw himself on his knees before Francis, begging admittance into their brotherhood. St. Francis accepted him lovingly.

Brother Elias, as this man came to be known in the order, joined the others on their walk. He was more a scholar, really, than one dedicated to a life of prayerful worship. In later years he became the general of the Franciscan Order, from which time onward his love of analysis undermined much of the free and spontaneous spirit that had marked the Order during the early period of its history.

On this particular day, however, he expatiated enthusiastically to the others on the reasons he'd decided to join them, and on the importance of the Order to the society of their time.

The friars had been singing as they walked. All of a sudden, their singing died in their hearts. They continued their walk in an uneasy silence.

Who would kill the song in a child's heart? Instead of explaining the benefits of living harmoniously, why not get the children simply to do whatever will help them to live in harmony with themselves and with others? Action, far more than words, will uplift them into a positive outlook.

Singing, too, is a wonderful therapy. No need to explain to a child the *reason* singing is therapeutic. Just get him to sing. In music lies one of the best ways of bringing out the best in children.

Dance is another excellent way. Body movements are closely allied to attitudes of the mind.

It might also help children to make affirmations while moving their bodies. They can walk vigorously in place, for example, affirming as they do so, "I am awake and ready!" Next, get them to stretch their arms out—first sidewise, then in front of them, then high above their heads, affirming, "I am positive—energetic—enthusiastic!" They can rub the palms of their hands vigorously over their bodies while affirming, "Awake! Rejoice, my body cells!" Next, tell them to rub their heads lightly with their fingertips, repeating, "Be glad, my brain! Be wise and strong!"

They can use the centering movements of dance to affirm, "I live in peace at the center of my being."

Certain outward-reaching dance movements might be used with the affirmation, "I reach out with love to help my fellow creatures."

Upward-stretching movements might be accompanied by the affirmation, "I reach up to the heights within myself."

Downward gestures could accompany the affirmation: "I reach down to uplift all who weep."

Vigorous dance steps and gestures might be accompanied by such words as, "Though troubles threaten me, I overcome them all!"

Certain yoga postures also, with related affirmations, are notably calming and invigorating to the entire body.

Painting, too, can be a means of drawing out feelings in a child which, once objectified, might be emphasized if the feelings are constructive, or positively redirected if they are destructive.

To share together in any activity, moreover, can help to harness excess energy and direct it positively.

A final word: Never underestimate the importance of fun to the over-all teaching process. It is often during the moments of lightness, when the mind is diverted, that the most fundamental lessons are absorbed.

Chapter 10

True Education Is Self-Education

It has been well said that a truth cannot be learned: It can only be recognized.

As I stated earlier, it isn't realistic to ask a child to determine what he shall learn. Mature decisions cannot be made in ignorance of the facts. But this much having been said, it remains equally true that unless the child also *wants* to learn, no amount of teaching will ensure that he absorbs anything. Effective teaching requires the student's willing cooperation. This willingness must be enlisted; it cannot be commandeered.

Thus, whatever system of education one follows, it must be flexible enough to provide for the shifting needs of a large variety of students. *It must be child-oriented.* A teacher may have specific information that he wants to impart, but if his students are not ready to receive it, his immediate job must be either to help them to receive it, or else to teach them what he thinks they *can* receive.

One of the mistakes often made by teachers, and by lecturers in all fields, is a tendency to be satisfied if they can convince themselves rather than their audiences. A good talk, however, whether a class or a lecture, is always in a sense a dialogue, even if one person does all the speaking. The competent speaker will "listen," as it were, to his audience—to their thoughts, their unspoken questions—and will respond accordingly. The more intuitive he is, the greater his ability will be to sense their needs, both as a group and as individuals.

Groups often experience a shared awareness, to which the sensitive lecturer can respond by tuning in to it. Often, the larger the group, the stronger this shared awareness. In a lecture to 2,000 people there may be a greater sense of dialogue in this sense than in a lecture to only six persons.

This group awareness may be more difficult to achieve where little children are concerned, particularly if the discussion centers in abstract principles. Dialogue, in this case, must be more literally what the word itself implies. Indeed, during the early years of education, close attention should be paid to every child. Classes should, if possible, be kept small. Take care to observe individual reactions, and to note any method that works for engaging the child's attention and interest.

People, including children, fall generally into basic types according to their temperaments and inclinations. These types divide themselves into a primary focus on body-awareness, on the feelings and emotions, on the will, and on the intellect. Children who are focused on body-consciousness need a different emphasis from those who by nature are more thoughtful. Some children respond to appeals to their finer feelings, while others respond best when their will is challenged. Some children must have the logic of a request explained to them, while others respond only to firm orders. No single rule holds true for every child.

I remember my father once giving my brother and me a spanking for something we'd done wrong. Well, wrong in his adult eyes, but not in ours. As we boys saw it, we'd only been helping to beautify the bathroom with large stars that we'd scratched with a screwdriver into the newly painted walls.

My brother Bob, whose temperament was more naturally body-oriented than mine, took his spanking matter-of-factly, then ran off and forgot the whole episode.

My own nature, however, was more thoughtful; I liked to probe into the "whys" of things. To me, our action had been well intentioned and deserved to be considered as such. To be spanked for it seemed to me an outrage against all that was just.

Weeks later, I looked at my father accusingly. "Why did you spank me?" I demanded. To Dad's credit, he recognized immediately that he had been mistaken. He never spanked me again.

It would be helpful for the teacher or the school staff to prepare a file on every child, listing his salient traits, his reactions to discipline and instruction, and suggesting directions that might be taken in future for his personalized "Education for Life."

It is probable that the child will fall naturally into one or another of the four types suggested above: physical, emotional, will-oriented, or thoughtful, though no one is ever purely one or the other. Indeed, the complete human being is balanced in all four of these aspects, which comprise, as we shall see later, the basic "tools" we all have to work with as human beings: body, feelings, will power, and intellect.

Certain contrasts might be considered also. Is the child's nature expansive or contractive? outgoing or withdrawn? positive or negative? constructive or destructive? imaginative or literal-minded? creative or imitative? aggressive or passive? assertive or submissive?

People generally assume that it is better for a child in each of the above cases to possess the first quality, rather than the second. An extroverted child, for example, is considered better adjusted than one who is introverted. This assumption is too simplistic. Do they mean adjusted merely because the child is not sufficiently introspective to be conscious of his own shortcomings? But it is often to the introvert that people turn for meaningful communication. Creative geniuses, too, are often introverted.

In many of the paired qualities mentioned above, the second is not a defect, nor should it necessarily be transformed at all costs into its opposite quality. It may even prove a virtue, once it has been refined and its potentials fully explored.

Submissiveness, for example, more easily than aggressiveness, may be developed into willing cooperation. A literal mind may never create works of imagination, but it may easily be interested in the pragmatic sciences. Thus, a tendency toward literal-mindedness, which in some contexts is a defect, might in others be a virtue.

In all cases, it is important to work with the child's strengths, rather than concentrating on his weaknesses. Usually, he will respond far better to this positive approach.

In certain cases, the choice is obvious enough. Negativity and destructiveness, for example, are universally undesirable traits; no effort should be spared to redirect them more positively. In many other cases, however, the choice is less obvious, and sensitive insight is needed to deal with them wisely.

An obstacle to the very exercise of such discernment is one of the fundamental tenets of modern education.

Tenet? Call it a dogma, rather. There is today the peculiar conviction—which one challenges at one's peril—that human beings are born equal in every respect, including in their native abilities. Surely, the well-known dictum, "All men are created equal," cannot have been intended so literally. For it flies in the face of all experience.

It is one thing to say that all men are created equal before God; or that all, in their shared humanity, have an equal right to rise to their own levels of competence, to develop their own talents, and to fulfill their reasonable desires according to their own intrinsic abilities. It may even be justifiable, philosophically speaking, to say that all men have the *potential* to attain to equal heights.

It is quite another thing, however, to say that all men are, at all times, equally competent, talented, and capable of achieving success. Anyone can see that this is not the case. How intelligent people can so blind themselves to a reality so self-evident is a commentary on the intellect's capacity for self-deception. Only a person thoroughly convinced that there are no sow's ears, only silk purses, could even contemplate such an absurdity.

Worse than the error itself—after all, we all do make mistakes—is the widespread envy that this error has produced. Can you even count the number of times you've heard the claim: "I'm just as good as anyone else"?

Good at *what?* Or do the people who make this claim mean, simply, *good?* That is, do they consider themselves as virtuous as any saint, and possessed of no trait which, with some effort on their part, might be improved? Is the only reason other people have achieved greater success in life than they, or greater popularity, or more widespread influence in the world, simply that those others have had all the luck? Have Certain Persons in High Places—envious of the sterling worth of these grumblers—withheld from them their deserved opportunities?

What foolishness!

Yet, the numbers of people who subscribe to this foolishness are legion. And they are responsible for much of the anger and hostility in our times.

In the classrooms, the tendency to equate equality with uniformity has led to the penalizing of brilliance, and to the careful nurturing of mediocrity.

Modern teaching is supposedly geared to the average student. (In this sense a sop is thrown, though hardly as a gesture of respect, to the principle of "listening" to the students.) But it is a surrender to perceived necessity. No one ever thinks in terms of *raising* the quality of teaching to an average level. The very emphasis on bringing everything to an average level suggests a *downward* direction. Once this downward direction is established, the tendency is to continue it further, toward the less-than-average students.

Many well-meaning teachers end up devoting a disproportionate amount of their attention to the dullest pupils, giving more or less perfunctory attention, in the process, to children even of average intelligence, and virtually none to the brilliant students. The brilliant ones, consequently, are deprived of challenges, and become bored. Often it is these last who become the "problem" children in the schools.

What is the result, finally? Modern education prepares people well enough for reading the headlines, but it leaves them more or less at a loss when confronted with a book. Instead, television gives them their intellectual fare.

Intelligence is only one standard of a student's all-round qualifications, of course. But it is obvious that all students are not equally intelligent. Neither are they all equally sensitive, creative, receptive, energetic, willing, or, in fact, equally *anything*. In a world where no two thumbprints are alike, the variety of human capabilities may be described as infinite.

Can we point, then, to progressive *levels* of development in these capabilities? In the case of intelligence, such a progression is more or less discernible. But what is needed also is a general criterion that will be helpful in developing all aspects of a child's nature.

Chapter 11

Progressive Development

A friend of mine one day, struggling in the quicksands of a negative mood, was attempting to define everything in life in terms of the general hopelessness of it all. He challenged me to say something that would make him see things differently. And of course, though I tried, my best efforts proved unavailing. For when a person *wants* to be unhappy, no one in the world can make him happy.

But then an inspiration came to me. "I'm not really worried about you," I said. "We all have a certain specific spiritual gravity, and return to it repeatedly and naturally after any period of temporary depression or euphoria. All that's required is that we relax into ourselves again. Your own specific gravity," I said, "is high. I'm sure you'll return to it naturally in a day or two without any help from me."

And so it proved.

It was a useful inspiration. In the world of physics, objects rise or sink, as we all know, according to their own specific gravity relative to the density of the medium surrounding them. A child's balloon, if filled with helium, will rise as soon as the child releases it, and will continue rising until its own specific gravity is the same as that of the atmosphere around it. An object placed in water will sink if its specific gravity is greater than that of water, but will float if it is less.

People too, I've noticed, sink or rise in their consciousness according to another kind of "specific gravity." Some natures are naturally heavy; others, naturally light.

People with a naturally positive outlook may rise above even extraordinary set-backs—tests under the impact of which other people, more pessimistically inclined, might sink without a trace.

There were prisoners in the German concentration camps of World War II whose positive outlook lifted them above that human tragedy. The very effort to remain positive brought them to greatness; they became deeply compassionate, forgiving, and wise.

On the other hand, it is not unusual to encounter people who complain unceasingly of their lot in life— not necessarily because their lot is hard, but merely because they are bored.

"Specific gravity" in human beings is what makes them, to varying degrees, positive or negative. To describe these differences in terms of "light" or "heavy" may be novel, but it is nevertheless apt. For the description addresses a subjective awareness that we all share. Indeed every language, as far as I know, contains words and expressions that describe positive and negative states of mind in terms of this specific gravity. We speak of feeling "high," "uplifted," or as if (to use the modern expression) "sailing on cloud nine." Or else we moan that we feel "low," "downcast," or "in the dumps." No one who feels spiritually heavy is likely to say, "I'm so happy!" A happy feeling is marked by a rising awareness—from heaviness toward a consciousness of lightness and expansion.

This metaphor can be applied to human development on every level. For it is literally true that certain qualities—laziness, for example, or envy—pull even the energy of the body downward in the spine, and that certain other qualities—kindness, or a spirit of willingness—lift it upward.

Perhaps, if we study personality traits in this context, we'll discern a universal kind of progression that will serve teachers well in their guidance of children.

The important thing will be to see whether the *specific* gravity—the long-term reality in this context, and not merely the passing moods—of a child can be improved, or "lightened." It is with this basic nature that the teacher should be especially concerned.

Let us consider some of the contrasting qualities mentioned in the last chapter. To refresh your memory, here they are again:

1. expansive vs. contractive;
2. outgoing vs. withdrawn;
3. positive vs. negative;
4. constructive vs. destructive;
5. imaginative vs. literal-minded;
6. creative vs. imitative;
7. aggressive vs. passive;
8. assertive vs. submissive.

Eight pairs of qualities. None of these qualities is static or absolute. They represent a progression, or a regression, in one of two directions, upward or downward.

The first pair of qualities—expansive vs. contractive—gives us our best clue as to how to apply this concept of "specific density" to human temperament generally. A helium-filled balloon rises. A stone sinks to the bottom of a lake. The difference between the gravity of helium and that of a stone lies simply in their specific density.

Similarly, when human consciousness is expansive it is "light"; when it is contractive, it is "heavy." An expansive, and therefore light, temperament, when faced with a problem, views it from a naturally broad perspective and is likely, in consequence, to be solution-oriented. A contractive, and therefore heavy, temperament is likely to see the problem itself as the entire reality. Contractive people are problem-oriented.

Imagine human consciousness as consisting of countless microscopic particles, like the motes of dust in a sunbeam. These motes, if they coalesce, may become solid lumps of earth. Imagine them, then, as "particles" of consciousness, light when their mass is widely dispersed, but heavy when they are compacted into a single "lump" of ego-consciousness. Expansiveness comes with sympathetic acceptance of the realities of others. With expansiveness, the "particles" of consciousness rise, even as a balloon rises upward, lifting one into an ever-lighter, more joyful outlook.

The more a person's sympathies expand to embrace family and friends, neighbors, country, mankind, all creatures, the more the "particles," so-called, of his consciousness become light in their expansiveness. The result is an ever-freer state of awareness.

Selfish people are "heavy" because of their self-involvement. Selfish people, moreover, in their heaviness of temperament, are habitually unhappy, negative, and morose. By contrast, unselfish people are habitually cheerful and positive.

The cure for unhappiness and negativity, then, is not, as selfish people imagine, to increase their concern for their own welfare. It is to *forget* themselves in concentration on the welfare of others.

Since not all children are easily motivated toward self-improvement, the solution is to surround them, as much as possible, with others of "lighter" consciousness than their own.

The great diversity of psychological traits all have in common this one, simple phenomenon of "specific gravity," or psychological "density." Expansiveness, happiness, and a positive outlook manifest lightness of spirit. Contractiveness, unhappiness, and negativity manifest heaviness of spirit.

It would, however, be simplistic to describe all the qualities contrasted above as either light or heavy. Take another pair: an outgoing nature vs. one that is mentally withdrawn. Superficially—and so might the judgment be in any popularity contest—it may seem that an outgoing nature is by very definition expansive, and a withdrawn nature, again by definition, contractive. If, however, we examine two children possessing one or the other of these traits from a point of view of their specific spiritual gravity, we may find that the appearance is deceptive.

For an outgoing nature is often egotistical and self-centered—seeking approval, recognition, and emotional support from others, rather than giving such support; a personality once described as, "Clap hands, here comes Charlie!" On the other hand, a withdrawn nature may be only contemplative, and not self-preoccupied at all, in its inner expansiveness enjoying an unusually light specific gravity.

It is from within, and not superficially from without, that each individual child must be understood.

Would, then, an outgoing but ego-centered nature fit into the same category of "heaviness" as one that was dull-minded and slothful? Hardly. There are relativities, in other words, of "lightness" and "heaviness." "Heavy" and "light," by themselves, are too broad as designations, too black and white; they don't account for in-between shadings of grey.

A third designation is needed, then, to cover these in-between states, and to explain shadings that express *more* light, or *more* darkness. An in-between designation would help, for example, to explain the difference between ego and egotism: between self-awareness and self-involvement. Human beings, whose developed awareness (compared to the lower animals) increases also their *self*-awareness, need this awakening to ego-consciousness as an incentive toward self-improvement. Self-involvement, however, obstructs self-improvement, for it blocks progressively rising states of awareness.

There is only one thing, really, that can lift a person out of the depths of spiritual unawareness—out of the relative "density" of dullness, laziness, and despair. It is not high-mindedness, to which quality dull minds cannot even relate. The bridge from mental dullness to higher awareness is constructed of intense activity of some kind. Of no use to the self-involved child are such expansive techniques as visualization, meditation, and positive thinking. None of these "light" activities can address the reality of a wholly negative attitude.

What, then, can help the spiritually "heavy" child to disperse his condensed aggregation of mental molecules? The answer is, by ego-motivated activity. We've described spiritual "density" as a contraction inward upon the ego. The way to lighten this density, then, will not be to deny the ego its accustomed satisfactions, but to suggest to the ego that it will find greater satisfaction in reaching outward to the world than in wallowing in self-involvement. The way to encourage a "heavy" child to break out of his mental enclosure of self-involvement is to provide him with incentives to become more outwardly active.

Outgoing, even if ego-affirming, activity is wholesome and positive for the contractive spirit.

This middle category, then, may be defined as *"ego-active."* Ego-centered activity can pull one in either of two directions—either toward further expansiveness, or toward a reaffirmation of contractiveness. We might therefore speak of these alternative directions as *"expansive ego-active"* and *"contractive ego-active."*

In expansive ego-activity there is a tendency toward progressive lightness, and a decreasing emphasis on the ego's importance.

In contractive ego-activity, on the other hand, though more expanded than the "heavy" quality of mental dullness, despair, and the like, the direction is still inward upon itself: toward the ego, in other words, as the center of awareness. Contractive ego-activity lacks the simplicity of clear purpose; in its restlessness it tends to kick up clouds of mental dust, obscuring anything to which the person gives his attention. His activity, like his consciousness, never produces truly beneficial results.

A child's nature can be gauged much more easily in these simple terms of his "specific spiritual gravity," or "density," than by pondering his psychological traits individually. In this simplicity lies a golden key with which to unlock the door to a child's spiritual maturity.

Like all simple methods, however, it requires sensitivity to use the key effectively. A bathroom scale cannot determine the weight in carats of a diamond. The relative spiritual density of a child cannot be gauged by a mind that is filled with prejudices. It can be gauged best by calm inner feeling, which is to say, by intuition. It is doubtful whether the process could be reduced to an objective science, for it depends too much on the perceptive sensitivity of the individual teacher.

Still, there are objective criteria that can help the sensitive teacher to arrive at insights that will help the child.

Heaviness or lightness in a child's consciousness will be revealed, for one thing, in the postures and movements of his body. A child with a "heavy" outlook will demonstrate that heaviness physically: in his posture, in the slump of his shoulders, in the curve of his spine. His gaze will be habitually downward. Even in the way he sits and walks, it will seem as though life were a burden to him.

A child of light consciousness, by contrast, reveals in his every gesture an inner spirit of lightness. You may see such a child raise his arms frequently, rather than letting them hang forlornly at his side, and square his shoulders instead of letting them sag. His sitting posture is upright, his gaze more habitually upward, and his walk energetic, not expressive of mental denial.

Again, a child's psychological "density" can be recognized in his choice of friends. Low-energy children will shun, and may even resent, children of high energy. The high-energy child, on the other hand, finds little to interest him in the company of children of low energy, and tends to seek as companions those whose energy level is as high as his own.

An exception to this rule is children who "mix downward" for special reasons—usually, though not always, to help their "heavier" companions.

Teachers may devise tests of a child's reactions to challenges. For instance, how readily does a child share his enjoyments with others? How truthful is he? Does he respond positively to discipline? When requested to do something, does he habitually seek excuses not to do it, or does he respond willingly? Does he show a sense of responsibility? Does he show initiative?

Observe him at play. Is he basically cheerful during moments of relaxation, or has he a tendency to be glum? Does he set himself in competition with others, or does he work with them in a cooperative spirit? On the other hand—another alternative—does he set himself apart from them; and, if so, does he seem to do so in a manner suggestive of self-enclosure and self-preoccupation, or does he keep to himself rather because the focus of his attention is elsewhere?

How can the teacher use this tool of specific gravity to help the child? As we have suggested, the first step is to gain a sensitive understanding of the child's "specific spiritual gravity," or normal level of awareness: from "heavy" through "ego-active" and finally to "light" consciousness. Gradations in between, and the question of whether the directional pull is upward or downward, will suggest themselves naturally.

Next comes motivating the children. How can the teacher get children to *want* to change their level of awareness, and to expand their self-identity? The answer is: Help them to understand that what is involved here is escape from pain on the one hand, and the discovery of happiness on the other. If they are already happy, they will already feel motivated to increase their happiness.

Specific methods for raising the child's level of awareness have been touched on lightly so far, and will be covered in depth in subsequent chapters.

How are these techniques to be used? Consciously, on the part of the teachers. Often, however, on the child's part, it would be as well for him not to be aware of the process, lest his self-consciousness spoil everything.

Other techniques, not mentioned elsewhere, include deep breathing. For in deep breathing the lungs become, as it were, a magnet to draw the energy up from the lower parts of the body.

Wholesome exercise is invigorating also, and will help children to awaken a flow of energy in the body. By directing this energy outward, it will be prevented from being turned inward, contractively.

Other techniques will occur to the teacher as he develops these practices. For example, a school I attended for two years in England as a boy had an ingenious system for inspiring us to make a greater personal effort. We were graded not only on our studies, but also on how hard we'd tried. This second grading system was done with colors. "Excellence" in this department was indicated by a double red oblong; "very good," by a single red oblong; "good," by a double green; "fair," by a single green. "Poor" was indicated by a double blue, and "very poor," by a single blue. Somehow, we all worked much harder to receive pretty colors than we ever would have for numerical grades.

Try also, if possible, to help the child in his selection of companions. If you encourage him to associate with "lighter" children, however, it might be better not to explain to him your reasons for doing so, lest he resent the implied suggestion of condescension on the part of his companions.

Finally, remember the importance to the child of your own magnetic influence. Live as much as possible, yourself, on higher levels of awareness. The more expanded *you* are in your consciousness, the more expanded the children in your care will become.

Let me close this chapter with a fourth Law. I have already given three others in this book: Walters' Law of Dogmatic Proliferation, The Maturity Principle, and Yogananda's Law of Basic Motivation. This fourth law may be called "The Happiness Principle": *Happiness increases in direct proportion to the expansion of empathy, and in inverse proportion to the contractive density of self-affirmation.*

Chapter 12

Every Child an Einstein?

I remember practicing the piano assiduously as a child, for hours at a time. I enjoyed it, though I can't say I came within even hailing distance of the child prodigies around. My mother, however—bless all mothers!—used to tell me, "If you want to, there's nothing to stop you from becoming a concert pianist."

What mother wouldn't like to believe that her little Jimmy might prove a prodigy, or someday become President, another Michelangelo, a famous scientist, or a great saint?

But—well, let's face it: How likely is it?

Every teacher worthy of the name, too, would like to be able to inspire his students to rise to the heights of fame and success.

But, well, again, let's face it: How likely is it?

The problem isn't only that there are few great people born in any age. Much worse: Our educational system actively *discourages* children from aspiring to greatness.

To begin with, the premise of the system is that the dullest student is entitled to exactly the same education as the brightest. No one, of course, would want to deny that opportunity to anyone. The problem lies in forcing it on children who neither want it nor are capable of responding to it with that recognition which is the essence of successful education.

It takes little to inspire a child of "light specific gravity" to soar. Considerably greater effort is needed to get an "ego-active" child to inch his way upward. And for anyone whose "specific gravity" is really heavy, even massive efforts may hardly budge him at all. To devote all one's energy toward making those heroic efforts is to exhaust one's own faith, finally, in the higher potentials of education.

One must do one's best, of course, for every student. Indeed, even dull students may succeed remarkably, occasionally. For human beings are a mixture of so many traits. A child with the heaviest consciousness may possess some vital, self-expanding trait by which, if emphasized, he might rise high above anyone's expectations of him. Normally, however, a spiritually heavy child can be helped most by recognizing and accepting, first, that his actual response to situations, however unnatural it may seem to the teacher, is natural for *him.*

Moreover, we need to ask ourselves: Is teaching a dull child to read the headlines, for example, the lofty success to which we want to point in justification of our entire educational system? Is it to be our only boast that we've transformed a few of our dull students into useful members of society? It would be desirable also, surely, to be able to point to the geniuses we've produced—especially if, in the process of producing them, we didn't penalize the dull.

What happens, instead, is that we handicap the bright students, and don't give even the mediocre ones that kind of education from which they might derive the most benefit.

Brightness suffers, but so also does society as a whole. For the world needs greatness in a few, at least, of its men and women, and is deprived when the system it fosters is prejudicial to the development of greatness.

Schools ought indeed to try to bring out the best in every child. But that "best" should be encouraged also as a quality distinct from its individual expression, and the potential for it recognized in those vehicles which are the most adapted to its fullest expression. I've mentioned genius, for example. It would be praiseworthy, no doubt, to encourage the manifestation of genius in a dull student, but where genius itself is concerned it would be more realistic to expect its manifestation in the bright ones. Instead, owing largely to an emphasis on merely discouraging the worst in children, what we often get in fact is the worst side of those children who have the highest potentials. That which is made the focus of one's concentration is usually what one achieves: not, in this case, discouragement of the worst, but rather affirmation of the worst.

It is never easy for a bright teacher to accept that dull children really *are* dull. But facts cannot be dealt with constructively so long as they are denied. Moreover, although it is always touching to read of a dull child who has been raised to normal functioning ability, the best way to help even that child is to give him the special focus he needs, without the teacher him- or herself having to feel inwardly divided by responsibility, within the same context, for the brighter pupils. These realities, though not of our choosing, are forced upon us by human nature itself. If we lack the courage to accept them, and to accept others as they *are* instead of as we wish they were or think they *ought* to be, we will be unable to help any of them with full effectiveness. It is, perhaps, "politically incorrect" to express such thoughts nowadays, but society cannot but depend to a disproportionate degree on its capable few to develop and flourish. As for the majority who lie between the polar opposites of brilliant and dull, they also thrive far better when their highest potentials are emphasized for them, and not minimized by emphasis on the lowest common denominator in the classroom.

A child who is "heavy" in terms of his specific spiritual gravity is likely to be dull-witted, slow, and more focused on using his body than his mind. How to inspire him to change? He probably isn't even interested in self-improvement. Try to expand his sympathies and you'll probably find that he thinks in terms, rather, of what others are or are not doing for him or giving him.

Even one such child in a classroom can drag the over-all level of teaching downward. If the child is ignored, on the other hand, or teased by his fellow students for his slow wit, he may gang up with others of similarly "heavy" consciousness to create trouble for everyone else in the school.

The "heavy-gravity" student may be inspired toward ego-motivated action. Never, however, until he is firmly established on an ego-active level, will he rise, except by sporadic bursts, to the kind of activity that is unselfishly motivated.

The best the teacher may accomplish with such a student is to teach him by means of a rudimentary system of punishment and reward: "Don't do that *if you know what's good for you*"; or, "Do that, and I'll buy you something good to eat." In this way, a few good habits may be inculcated into him that will stand him in good stead later in life, even if he isn't quite sure how or why they're right.

All this, however, is compromise. The basic problem remains: How to educate everyone without depriving anyone of the best education he can absorb? Is the answer to have separate classrooms—even separate schools? Is it to have separate grading systems, *A* to *D,* for each classroom or for each school, with sub-classifications indicating in which division the pupil has studied?

These are possible solutions. For present purposes, however, they seem remote and impracticable.

There is another, and also better, solution. It is suggested by the old country school house, where one teacher had to instruct multiple grades. There was only one way that that system could be made to work: The teacher had to enlist the help of the older students in instructing the younger ones.

The difference, in the present context, is that we are not dealing with one teacher for an entire school. It isn't a question, then, of older children teaching the younger. Rather, our concern is with students of the same age, but of diverse spiritual "densities."

My proposal concerns a shift of emphasis, of direction. At present, the view is from below upward, in the sense of bringing the low students up to a level where, it is hoped, all will be able to move onwards together.

Here, then, is the proposal: Instead of working *upward* from below, why not work *downward* from above?

How? Quite simply, by enlisting the help of "lighter" students to uplift the "heavier."

We have already seen that ego-active students may voluntarily mix with those of "heavy" consciousness, and that "light" students, similarly, may mix with ego-active students. The motive in both cases is usually not so much the gratifications of a friendly rapport as it is to help those below them.

"Heavy" students generally show little inclination in any case to listen to their teachers. But they will often listen to, and follow, children of their own age who are more aware, and more magnetic, than themselves. And whereas ego-active students may be more prone than the "heavy" ones to heed the advice of their teachers, they, too, are inclined rather to follow their more magnetic peers.

If the "heavier" member of such an association is even slightly receptive, the magnetic exchange between him and the more positive student may help to draw him up the ladder toward a higher "specific gravity."

In the context of an Education for Life system, moreover, the student of relatively expansive awareness actually gains by helping others of less expansive awareness than himself. It is not as though teaching the slow learner deprived him in his own studies. The more he shares with others the principles for better living that he has learned, the more he practices and strengthens his own awareness of those principles. In this way no one loses, and everyone gains.

It is ironic that the very students who are the most inclined to learn from their teachers, and the most capable of doing so, are generally those who, under the present system, receive the least from them.

What every teacher ought to do, instead, is assiduously cultivate leadership qualities in any student who shows an inclination to reach down and help others below him on the "ladder" to grow toward true emotional maturity.

There remains, of course, the danger of such students developing into "teachers' pets," and thus becoming universally shunned by the other students. But there are ways around this pitfall.

First, and most obviously, the teachers themselves should be trained to be aware of this danger, and to make their selections on an impersonal basis, perhaps also with the help of other teachers. Because human nature is weak, moreover, it won't suffice merely to admonish teachers to avoid the pitfall of favoritism.

Rather, students selected to help others should form councils of their own. "Light," or expansive, students should be given one emphasis in their leadership, and "ego-active" students another. Obviously, sensitive issues are raised here which can only be worked out in living situations, since these will change with every class.

The important thing is to realize that human magnetism is a fact of life. High-energy people *are* magnetic. And low-energy people invariably lack magnetism.

What do I mean by magnetism? Certainly I don't mean that a compass will veer from true north and point toward people of high energy! Still, magnetism is a fact of which everyone is aware, even if only dimly.

Such human magnetism might be compared to the magnetic field created when electricity flows through a copper wire. The higher the current, the stronger the electro-magnetic field. The higher the energy of a person, similarly, the greater his personal magnetism.

Much might be written on this subject. I myself have treated it at some length in others of my writings, and in a video recording, available through the publisher, titled "The Art of Magnetic Leadership." The important point here is for the teacher to realize that he will get nowhere at all if he encourages the merely "goody-goody" student to assume a leadership role. The child who is always prompt, willing, and supportive may seem at first the ideal choice. Unfortunately, such a child is often good merely because he wants ego-approval from the teacher, or because he lacks the strength of will to say what he really means. The best choice may well be one who occasionally gets into a little mischief himself. (I've always remembered the advice a wise woman saint in India gave to a child: "Be good, but not *too* good!")

Energy, then, must be included as a vital criterion. The child of low energy but of eternally good will is sure not to have the magnetism to attract and inspire others. Only in high-energy children can real leadership be developed.

And of course, high-energy students are among those the least likely to develop into teachers' pets.

Don't, therefore, seek out the "yes"-children to implement your programs. And don't be afraid at least to *consider* those of high energy who are slow to follow your directives. For these less malleable ones, once they've thought a proposal through, will often be those most dedicated to any responsibility they accept.

Avoid, like the poison it is, an over-emphasis on personalities. Concentrate always, rather, on principles.

And don't be afraid to pose challenges. A great weakness exhibited by many teachers is the tendency, in an effort to get the children on their side, to play up to them. If you will look back over your own school years, I think you will find that the teachers who were the most universally admired, even loved, by the students were those who were scrupulously fair, who stuck by their principles, and who never succumbed to the temptation to do something merely in the hope that they would be liked for doing it.

Children, themselves steeped in the immature ego's craving for acceptance by others, are highly sensitive to this weakness when they perceive it in adults. They quickly discern and despise it, especially so in their teachers, to whom they look for help in their own efforts to climb up the ladder to maturity.

Chapter 13

The Case against Atheism

In Queensland, Australia, a few years ago I was giving a seminar on some of the principles contained in this book. A man approached me afterwards.

"I entered the room toward the end of your talk," he said, "and heard you referring to God. Now then, I'm an atheist. How would you define God in a way that would be meaningful to me?"

I reflected a moment, then answered him, "Why not try thinking of God as the highest potential you can imagine for yourself?"

He stood there for a moment in surprise, then delivered his verdict: "Well now, that's a definition I can live with!"

Mankind *needs* something to look up to—an ideal, a dream, an aspiration. We may think of that ideal as God, forever *consciously* awaiting and encouraging us to seek Him. Or we may think of it as merely some goal held consciously in our own minds. In any case, the goal is, in a sense, conscious, for to us its attainment implies something to do with consciousness, a *conscious* fulfillment. It is no wooden idol, certainly.

So then, for heaven's sake, why *not* call it God?

Voltaire wisely said, "If God didn't exist, mankind would need to invent Him."

I'm not referring to a "God of the Christians," or a "God of the Jews." For that matter, within the actual body of worshiping Christians and Jews—and that goes equally for Hindus, Moslems, and the followers of every other religion—there are probably as many concepts of God as there are worshipers. The very word, *God,* is spoken merely by the tongue. It is doubtful that this word—in English, no less!—receives the same recognition elsewhere in the universe that we accord it ourselves.

Some people will imagine the Deity as Michelangelo's God, depicted on the ceiling of the Sistine Chapel at the moment of creating Adam. Others will imagine Him as Krishna smilingly playing the flute to attract souls away from the delusion of ego-attachment. To still others, "He" will be a "She": a Universal Mother. Again, to some, God will be an impersonal Light, or Love, or Absolute Consciousness.

People have fought wars over their definitions of God, not realizing that even within their own ranks there was never true unanimity of belief. For whatever words were used, the concept of each believer could only be the outcome of his own experience of life. And how can the experiences of any two people on earth be exactly alike?

I remember, when I was a young man, trying to visualize God as a Universal Mother. The thought of divine compassion as a feminine quality attracted me. I wasn't familiar with Roman Catholicism and its many images of the Madonna. The best I could come up with, eventually, was a mental image of my godfather's wife, a sweet-tempered, motherly lady, or at least one who had never been in the uncomfortable position of having to discipline me.

Will somebody scold me as a blasphemer for holding such a human concept? You see, I knew perfectly well that "Aunt Anna," as I called her, wasn't God. It was just that thinking of her helped me to conjure up in my own mind the qualities of kindness and compassion on which I wanted to concentrate. In prayer I eventually passed beyond this mental image to a sense of something more "acceptable"—a higher, omnipresent, ever-listening Presence.

The point is that even though no mental concept could ever fully define God, this doesn't mean that we ought therefore to abandon mental concepts altogether and get on with the prosaic job of gathering in facts, facts, and more facts, like so many bundles of sheaves. (Odd, is it not? that professors who so love every sort of intellectual theory will generally avoid any mention of a concept of the Divinity—because, they explain, it is "only" a theory!)

I am not offering God as a theory, however, but as a universal need. "God" is, if you like, only a word. But what this word stands for is the universal desire of human beings to be inspired; to experience a higher reality than that of a full belly; to be lifted above the heavy mud of unknowing into the free sky of an expanded, ever-lighter awareness. It is a need most of us recognize, and all of us know on deeper-than-conscious levels of our being. Why quibble, then, about the mere word?

The problem is that the whole bias of modern thinking, and therefore of modern education, is, as we saw in the last chapter, toward the depths. Science came along a few centuries ago and said, "Look, we can't prove the existence of God, or of heaven, or of angelic beings. But we *can* prove mass, weight, and motion. So let us stick with these." Some of those scientists were in fact devout religious believers. They were only trying to evolve a new approach to reality, based on provable facts.

The idea they proposed was excellent. Moreover, it is amazing how vast and complex scientists have discovered the universe to be after four hundred years, merely as a result of this seemingly simplistic approach to reality. Science has shown us a universe of hundreds of billions of stars and galaxies—a picture of things that would have been dismissed as the ravings of a lunatic had it been suggested even as recently as a century ago!

In leaving God out of scientific reckoning, however, the impression conveyed, now that scientists have won the day for their scientific method, is that God should be left out of *all* sensible reckoning, even when dealing with non-material issues. It was said once, "The only fit study for mankind is man himself." Today this maxim has undergone a complete change. The new study fit for mankind is expressed more or less thus: "The only fit study for mankind is the quantification of material phenomena by the sciences of physics and chemistry."

Darwin claimed that man is "descended," in a manner of speaking, from the monkeys. People in Darwin's day were already schooled to think of matter, not man, as the proper study of mankind. And then Darwin's claim caused people to see themselves as a mere coalescence of material atoms—a product, through a process of purely accidental selection, that we are pleased to consider intelligent and "civilized."

Freud, following this natural ideological progression, explained human nature in terms of the basic sex drive, from which he ended up defining all of us in terms of various related abnormalities. Succeeding generations of psychologists sought to explain man in other simplistic terms, all of them related to our animal origins. Adler, for example, gave an equally Darwinian emphasis to the desire for power (a product, one assumes, of the Darwinian struggle for survival).

In these views, man is wholly identified with his lower nature, and is considered merely to gloss over this embarrassing fact when he pretends to possess ideals. According to such Darwin-inspired concepts, if anyone you know happens to believe in divine love, you'd be wise to consider protecting your daughters' virtue. For divine love is only a mask, favored by hypocrites, for the earthy lustfulness of a two-legged goat.

And then, for that matter, why even bother to protect your daughter? If our only reality *is* our lower nature, why not with Sartre, and in the modern vernacular, "go for it"?

Modern education, whether consciously or unconsciously, is founded on this bottoms-up view of things. And the churches have made the worst possible case for their higher counsel by losing their tempers and hurling anathemas, by insisting that we are all sinners anyway (so why not "sin away" with the worst of them?), and by insisting on substituting definitions— dogmas, that is—for reality. They've given the educators the best imaginable excuse for *not* including God in the classroom. For religionists everywhere shout: "*This* is what God is!" "No, no, you fool, He is *that!*" Anyone in search of truth is likely to end up declaring in disgust, "A plague on both your houses!"

Scientists at least agree that the sun and moon are more or less what they can be observed to be. With so much disagreement in the churches, why *should* the schools deal with a subject that even churchmen can't agree on, and that is, evidently, unteachable?

And yet, our children cannot but yearn for something more than sterile facts. They yearn to be told that there is indeed something worthwhile in which to believe and toward which to aspire. Yes, they yearn for ideals.

Knock out the concept of God and you knock out the very basis of civilization. For you knock out the fundamental hope for human betterment.

We have already seen that moral and spiritual values need not be confined to any sectarian teaching. Humility, for example, is quite unnecessarily called *Christian* humility. Humility is humility, simply. Our understanding of this quality is merely hampered by the additional label "Christian."

Why can't we do the same thing with the concept of God? Why plaster our concept of him with the various labels that religionists have given Him, along with their claim to speak on His behalf?

Why speak of a "Christian" God, or a "Jewish" God? Why not consider the possibility that there might even be an "atheists' God"?

For though the atheist claims to reject God altogether, all he is really rejecting is definitions of God. For himself, he *must* be motivated by some ideal, some goal, some principle, or else abandon his very humanity. And that principle, for him, is what others call God, for it is the highest point toward which he himself can presently aspire.

Granted, one person's ideals may not be another person's. Yet I venture to say that there is *no* principle that the human mind, limited as it is, can conceptualize that can hold up its head and claim with conviction, "In this principle, finally, lies an absolute definition of God!"

In 1960 I was one of the speakers at an interfaith conference in Calcutta, India. It had been organized by a young and idealistic Jain monk who wanted to get representatives of the major world religions to agree on a set of tenets that would enable them to present a united front against the perceived threat of materialism.

Instead, the delegates used the conference as a platform to declaim on whatever beliefs seemed to separate them one from another.

As they spoke, I found myself imagining them trying actually to agree on even one universal tenet. Clearly, it would not be easy.

One of them might propose as self-evident to the followers of any religion the simple belief in God. But to this proposal, the Buddhists would object. For Buddhism is atheistical.

Well, then, what about getting everyone to agree that life continues after death? Here, too, certain religions would have to abstain.

In the nineteen-fifties, John Ball, the author, made a study of the major world religions, and found only one point on which all of them were in agreement: Every religion, he pointed out, teaches some variant of the Golden Rule: "Do as you would be done by." It was an interesting study, though it left me thinking, "And for this we need *religion?*"

The Golden Rule seems little more than the sort of solution that any civilized human being would discover on his own as a result merely of living in the society of others. It is a philosophy, in other words, of enlightened self-interest. It would have been strange indeed if the great religions had not included some variant of this statement in their teachings.

But there is, in the world's great religions, a higher teaching also. For all of them endeavor to inspire man in some way toward higher consciousness—in other words, toward a less "dense" awareness in the sense suggested in these pages, toward becoming less ego-centered, and more self-expansive. This is not, perhaps, a stated *tenet* in all the world religions, but it is certainly a universal effect experienced by anyone who sincerely lives by their teachings.

Even Shintoism, a Japanese ceremonial religion which more or less limits itself to marrying and burying its adherents, offers them in the process a sense of the harmony and fitness of things, and, as such, fosters a *consciousness* of harmony: one aspect, surely, of an uplifted awareness.

It is time, and long past time, that we reinstituted in the schools an emphasis on high values and high ideals. Indeed, the process of evolution—both of species, outwardly, and of individuals, inwardly—is not only a push upward from below, but also a magnetic appeal from above.

Science speaks of energy in both potential and kinetic states. Both states are real, though in its potential form the energy is not yet overtly manifested. Why dismiss human potentials, then, as non-existent? The very fact that they *are* potentials makes them real, in a sense, even now. If they were not potential, moreover, they could never become manifested. It is not only the push of the struggle for survival that moves us upward toward perfection: It is an attraction, recognized universally on deeper-than-conscious levels of our being, toward a state that we know to be true and natural to ourselves.

Mankind is not seduced from reality by his dreams of beauty and perfection. Rather, the greatest accomplishments are achieved by those who dare to cherish such dreams. For once the stomach has been filled, the body clothed, and one's living space insulated against the elements, there remains a basic hunger in us all which no amount of possessions, power, or pleasure can fulfill: the need to know and to understand, to participate with wonder in the great adventure of existence in this universe.

Children cannot be forced to learn. And mankind cannot only be pushed up the ladder toward final awakening. We must be attracted upward by the response of our free will.

That magnet, finally, which has ever drawn humanity upward is what people define in their minds—dimly still, perhaps, but let us hope with growing comprehension—as God.

Chapter 14

The Tools of Maturity

An astronomer scanning the heavens needs a mirror for his telescope that is clean and ground accurately. A carpenter building a house needs tools that are well made and well maintained. A jeweller dealing in precious stones needs a scale sensitive enough to weigh small fractions of a carat. In every department of life, the right tools are needed. In this age of sophisticated technology, especially, great care must be devoted to their development and maintenance.

It is a matter for surprise, then, how little attention gets paid to the ultimate "tool," the one on which every human being relies: his own self, his body and his brain.

The physical body, if not treated sensitively and with proper awareness, can end up becoming man's own worst enemy. An ill body can obstruct every effort of the will toward accomplishment. A brain that is clouded, unfocused, or easily overwhelmed by emotional stress understands nothing clearly no matter how excellent the material instruments a person uses.

Our modern school system concentrates on imparting facts, but devotes far too little attention to developing a student's ability to *absorb* the information he receives. It gives him the outer tools for accomplishment, but never even suggests to him methods for developing his powers of concentration, his memory, his ability to think clearly, without which those tools are like a hammer and saw in the paws of a cat.

In one of my classes when I was schoolboy, if any student seemed unable to grasp the point under discussion the teacher would inquire with jocular solic- itude, "What's the matter, Jones [or Smith, or Robbins]? Are you in love?" Strange to say, this was the only recognition the student ever received of the possible importance of his emotions to the total learning process.

Even in such basic matters as diet, how much are our children taught? They are given (for one example) what has come to be called "junk" food, high in sugar content and low in nutritive value. Does no one ever tell them that too much sugar clouds the mind, making it difficult to think clearly? or that nutritious food will help them to feel better in all departments of their lives? Fortunately, people *are* becoming more conscious in these matters nowadays, though the great majority are still either ignorant or indifferent to the discoveries being made in this field.

Exercise

In matters of physical exercise, children are invited to engage in violent sports that will stand them in no useful stead later in life, and that in some cases perma- nently injure their bodies. But how much attention is paid to teaching them forms of exercise that will benefit them throughout their lives?

Exercise should be approached in the manner of a long distance runner, with clear recognition given to the fact that the physical body may have to serve its owner for another seventy, eighty, or more years, and ought not to be treated as though the exercise it is getting now will end with graduation.

A young friend of mine, an excellent skier, used to enjoy making jumps that, because of her skill, she survived splendidly, but that jarred every bone in her body. Wisely, she abandoned the practice when her physician told her, "If you go on like this, by the time you're forty-five you'll be confined to a wheel chair."

Children would soon become bored, of course, if all the exercise they were permitted was a daily trudge around the compound. I'm not recommending tiresome exercise. Even walking and hiking, however, can be enjoyable when pursued in the broad, open countryside, inhaling fresh air and feasting the gaze on green fields and hills.

The will needs challenges, too, if it is to grow strong. In this sense, certainly, strenuous sports play a definitely useful role in education. What I am pleading for, then, is the addition of common sense, a view to life's longer rhythms, and physical development and the sorts of exercise that will stand the child in good stead later in life even if they don't make him the hero of an hour.

Here's an example of the importance of physical exercise: The other day my brain was feeling foggy, no doubt from over-work. No amount of flogging it with affirmations of energy could get it to stagger out into the sunlight of clear thought. I left my desk, therefore, and jogged for ten minutes on a trampoline. The difference, afterward, in my mental clarity was amazing.

A steady routine of exercise is important for everyone—exercise that doesn't require a football field and two teams to bludgeon one another into semi-paralysis, but that is pleasant and even fun to engage in. This habit should be inculcated in children, even in those with a greater fondness for intellectual pursuits.

Good diet, right exercise, regular exposure to sunlight and fresh air: These can develop the body as a tool for the long-range efficiency of the whole being.

The Emotions

Then there is the question of the emotions. How many adults, what to speak of children, recognize the difference between emotion and feeling? Very few.

And how many children, consequently, are taught that calm, sensitive feeling is an invaluable tool for the complete understanding of most subjects? Or that *turbulent* feelings—that is to say, the emotions—and not feeling *per se* prevent clear, objective understanding? Again, very few.

Few children, again, are taught the extent to which reason is guided by calm feeling, but distorted by the emotions. And few are taught that by developing calm feeling they will improve their understanding of objective reality on every level.

Feeling, when it is calm and refined, is essential both to truly objective and to mature insight.

There are ways of clarifying feeling, just as there are principles of logic (already taught in the schools) for learning to reason correctly. Feeling can be clarified, for instance, by learning how to distance feeling from one's personal likes and dislikes, withdrawing one's awareness to a calm center in the heart. Feeling can be clarified by directing the heart's energies upward to the brain, and thence to a point between the eyebrows that was anciently identified as the seat of concentration in the body. Clarity of feeling can be assisted by calming the flow of energy in the spine, by means of certain breathing exercises. These exercises are a priceless contribution of the science of yoga to the general knowledge of the human race. It would be a grave error to ignore them on the grounds of one's unfamiliarity with them.

Only by calm inner feeling can a person know definitely the right course to take in any action. Those who direct their lives from this deeper level of feeling achieve levels of success that are never reached by people who limit their quest for answers to the exercise of reason. Reason, indeed, if unsupported by feeling, may point in hundreds of plausible directions without offering certainty as to the rightness of any of them.

Children need to learn how to react *appropriately.* This they can never do if their reaction springs out of their subjective emotions. Considerable training is needed to learn how to harness feeling and make it a useful ally. What children are taught, instead, as they grow older, is that feelings are inevitably obstacles to correct insight. The scientific method is offered as a model. "If you want to see things objectively," they are told, "you must view everything in terms of cold logic." I remember a professor when I was in college who boasted, jokingly, that x-rays had shown his heart to be smaller than normal. This, to him, was a sign of intellectual objectivity, which he prized.

Ignored is the fact that, usually, the greater the scientist, the more deeply he *feels* his subject. Or that, as Einstein put it, the essence of true scientific discovery is a sense of mystical awe.

Feeling can never in any case be suppressed. Shove it out of sight at one point—where you can at least see it and try to deal with it—and it will only pop up at another, often a place where you least expect it. Many times, when long-suppressed feelings have at last burst upon people's consciousness, those feelings have assumed terrible and unrecognizable shapes. Sometimes they have actually incited to riot.

Right feeling is an important tool for achieving maturity. It must be cultivated, and not merely ignored, suppressed, or treated as something about which nothing "reasonable" can be done.

Will Power

A third tool of maturity is *will power.*

Every year, hundreds of businesses are started, only a few of which ever succeed. Are the rare success stories due only to "the luck of the draw"? Are the businesses that fail merely victims of "negative statistics"? The one thing that stands out in every success story is the extraordinary *will power* it required.

The one trait which all successful people have in common is that they can't even imagine saying, "I can't." If one method doesn't work, they'll try another, and if not that, then still another. They'll keep on trying until they find something that does work.

How often people lose courage after one or two half-hearted attempts! And how often they imagine a job to be finished after they've only talked about it, or outlined it on paper. How often, again, do people give up after encountering a mere sprinkling of obstacles, offering the excuse, "It wasn't meant to be."

Business colleges fill their students' brains with marketing techniques, organizational charts, and secrets of profitable investment. They send graduates out into the world in the belief that all this knowledge will be their guarantee of success. How is it, the graduates wonder later on, that so few of them make the grade?

Even more incomprehensible to them is the large number of highly successful business people whose training couldn't compare with their own. How, for example, did that steel tycoon earn his millions? Good heavens, he never even finished *grade* school!

The answer is quite simple: He stuck to it. He made things happen, instead of waiting for circumstances to be just right for the application of principles he'd learned in school from others.

No one can really succeed in life who hasn't a strong will power. Will power, then, is a vital ingredient of maturity, and should be emphasized as such in the schools. Techniques should be taught for developing it, and opportunities explored for its expression.

The Intellect

The fourth, final, tool of maturity is the intellect. One may say, "Here, at least, is one faculty to which we need pay no special attention. Modern education is already fully devoted to its development."

Devoted, perhaps, but not with sufficient awareness of what it takes to bring the intellect to full development. For when intellect is treated as a thing apart from the other three tools of maturity—body, feeling, and will power—it grows like a poorly nourished and anemic plant. A plant may grow tall and yet be weak, colorless, and fragile.

One weakness of the intellect is, as we have seen, a tendency to soar up, up, and away like a balloon into clouds of fascinating theory, while carelessly discarding as unnecessary the weighty ballast of fact. A balanced awareness of the material realities that are experienced first of all through the physical body is necessary for the development of the intellect to its full usefulness.

Another weakness of the intellect is, as we have seen also, a tendency to substitute theory for action— even to consider itself betrayed by cloddish reminders of the very need for action. Regular, daily doses of will power are necessary to prevent this weakness from degenerating into mental paralysis.

A third weakness is—and here is where *feeling* shows its importance—the temptation of intellectuality to imagine that it is so clever that it can actually *create* truths. There comes upon certain people of exceptional intelligence a sort of Olympian delusion: the thought that, by the power of reason alone, they can demonstrate any rational conclusion they desire. Is it their wish to prove that black is white, or white, black? No problem! They imagine themselves capable of reasoning any truth into or out of existence, merely by the clever manipulation of ideas.

We see here, indeed, the danger of suppressing one's feelings: They only rise again, and again and again, as Michael Ende pointed out in *The Never-Ending Story,* in the form of the most fantastic lies.

Paramhansa Yogananda put it well when he wrote: *"Reason is rightly guided only when it acknowledges the inescapability of cosmic law"*—that is to say, the inescapability of what *is*.

Thus, the intellect must be developed in constant reference to demonstrable truths. Webs of logic finely spun out of nothing more substantial than an intriguing fancy, or a quotation, must be referred again and again to reality to see whether or not they really are true.

A further point is that the intellect needs to be developed along *useful* lines. Of what value, for example, a wonderful plan for battle that entails the deployment of ten thousand troops, when the only men one has at his disposal are a few foot-weary troops?

And what is the use of a doctor exclaiming proudly, "The operation was a success!" when the patient himself died peacefully on the operating table?

The intellect must be developed, finally, in full recognition that it is merely a tool wielded by the mind, but never itself fully in charge of the mind. Like any tool, it can be used rightly or wrongly, depending on one's respect for other, higher, and forever immutable principles.

Conclusion

A human being, in order to function fully and effectively in this world, needs to develop in himself all four of these tools of maturity: 1) physical energy and bodily self-control; 2) emotional calmness and expansive feeling; 3) dynamic, persistent will power; and 4) a clear-sighted, practical intellect. Remove any one of these aspects from the equation and the equation itself becomes distorted. Each aspect depends for its perfection on the other three.

A person of great physical energy and control, but with undeveloped feeling, will power, or intelligence, will be little more than a human animal, responding to every stimulus on a purely instinctual level.

A person of sensitively refined feelings, but underdeveloped in the other three aspects of maturity, will too easily lose himself in hypochondria or in other nameless fears.

A person, again, of strong will power, but deficient in the other three tools of maturity, may compensate for his physical weakness by developing a tyrannical nature. Lack of emotional control may plunge him into violent rages against anyone so presumptuous as to oppose him even on minor issues. And an undeveloped intellect may lead him to commit actions that are unbridled because never viewed in the light of calm introspection.

We have seen, finally, the deficiency of the intellect when it is unsupported by the other three "tools" of maturity.

An interesting point is that these tools are best developed in sequence: bodily awareness first, then sensitivity of feeling, then will power, and last of all, intellect.

Feeling, for example, needs grounding in a firm sense of physical reality if it is really to inspire and uplift the child instead of causing him to run maudlin. Will power, when developed without reference to both physical energy and controlled or wisely directed emotions, can lead to ruthlessness, or to fitful explosions of energy that serve no practical purpose.

In teaching a child, therefore, care should be taken not only to teach him the right use of his body, feelings, will power, and intellect, but also to lead him through their development in the proper sequence. Only by understanding and respecting his nature as it is can he be helped to achieve the equilibrium of true maturity.

Chapter 15

The Stages of Maturity

Certain medicines are designed to release their healing properties into the body gradually, a few hours at a time.

Certain changes in the human body, similarly, are programed to occur years apart in a person's life.

At about six years, the child begins to lose his baby teeth, substituting for them new teeth that will be suitable to an adult body. Roughly at twelve years, he undergoes the traumatic physical, mental, and emotional changes that come with puberty. At about eighteen years his body stops growing, and he prepares mentally for adulthood. Women at more or less forty-eight years enter menopause, often accompanied by mental and emotional upheavals.

The changes people undergo in their lives are not only physical. There is the well-known "mid-life crisis," for example. And there is the psychological need, around the age of sixty, to withdraw from outward activity. At thirty, or slightly earlier, people may begin at last to get a clear sense of their particular "mission" in life.

It has even been found statistically that certain mental abilities peak at different ages: mathematics and poetry, for example, during the late teens and early twenties; business acumen, in the fifties; philosophical insight, in the sixties and seventies.

The stages of life make a fascinating study. Various explanations have been offered for them. Astrologers, for example, relate the more significant of them to the cycles of Saturn and Jupiter: Saturn, for the cycles governing his outer life, including his life's work; Jupiter, for his inner development.

It may be only coincidence, but the twelve-year cycles of Jupiter—six years of movement away from the point of origin in the horoscope or birth chart, and six years of inward return—actually do correspond to certain developments in a person's life. If nothing else, they make a useful peg, at least, on which to hang our awareness of these developments.

In the life of a growing child, these stages are particularly noteworthy. For in the child's psychological and spiritual development there are four clearly marked stages, at each of which it becomes natural for him to assume responsibility for developing the next basic "tool" of maturity that I've described above.

The first six years of a child's life are taken up primarily with the development of physical awareness. The following six, until about the age of twelve, mark the natural period for developing emotional sensitivity. From twelve to eighteen, teenage rebelliousness is a natural symptom of a developing will power. And the last six years of these two twelve-year cycles, from eighteen to twenty-four, are the time of life when the intellect begins naturally to flower.

These four phases of development represent, as I said, the first two cycles of Jupiter in a person's life, each with an outward followed by an inward flow. Thus, the outward flow occurs during the first and the third cycles: bodily awareness and control in the first, and growing affirmation of the will in the third. The inward direction occurs during the second and the fourth cycles: emotional awareness and refinement from the ages of six to twelve, and intellectual awakening in the fourth, from eighteen to twenty-four.

If the reader should want a less exotic explanation than the twelve-year cycles of Jupiter, he may look instead to the correlation that exists between these four stages of maturity and fundamental changes that take place in the physical body: the appearance, at about six years of age, of the child's first permanent teeth; the advent of puberty at about the age of twelve; and the cessation of physical development at about the age of eighteen.

In whatever way one seeks to explain these four stages—even as convenient memory pegs, only—the stages are readily observable facts. Dismiss every theory, and the facts remain. They simply exist.

Friends of mine, who teach children the Suzuki method for learning to play the violin, have informed me that until the age of six their students are fully occupied with the sheer physical mechanics of playing. From six to twelve years, they are moved by the beauty of the music. And from twelve onwards, through high school, they labor determinedly at mastering technique.

The Physical Years

The first thing a baby needs to learn is how to cope with his body. At first he can only wave his arms and legs helplessly in the air. Then he begins to crawl, then toddle, then walk, and finally to run about enthusiastically. Even as late as his sixth year, the child is still physically awkward, colliding with things as he runs, dropping bottles if he removes their caps, and scattering food with his fork when feeding himself.

Beyond muscular control, the child's first six years are a time of sensory awakening to the world around him. Sights, sounds, smells, tastes, the tantalizing way things feel to the touch—all of these have, for him, an amazingly vivid reality. The rainbow colors of sunlight in a dewdrop; the distinctive tread of every member of his household; fragrant morning smells in the kitchen; the smooth feeling of clean sheets—these and countless other impressions flood constantly into his mind.

During these first years, then, with the child's developing sensory awareness, he can be taught most easily through his body and through bodily movement.

Then, at about the age of six, he is ready to be instructed through the medium of emotional awareness. This doesn't mean that he has been emotionally unaware until then—far from it! During his first six years, his subjective awareness may have seemed almost a cauldron of boiling emotions. After six, however, he comes to a time when it is possible for him to focus on directing and refining those emotions.

It is from this age onward, for example, that a child can be inspired to develop noble sentiments. This six-year period is a natural time for hero worship. It is also the best time, therefore, to offer him constructive role models—in legend, fantasy, history, and among presently living human beings.

The Willful Years

At twelve years, or thereabouts—that is, with the onset of puberty—the ego begins to assert itself more forcefully. With this assertion comes an awakened need to test and strengthen the will. The important thing, at this time, is to guide the adolescent toward the right use of his will power—that is to say, to use it expansively, not contractively. Especially important during these years is it for him to learn self-control. He should be encouraged to flex the "muscles" of his will power in constructive ways—not to try to dominate others, for example, or to prove himself in their eyes, but to learn that true greatness means being a bulwark of strength for others.

Bodily awareness during the teen-age years assumes new meaning, and must be channeled healthfully, especially into sports and other vigorous forms of exercise. The teenager must learn also how to channel his physical energies creatively, toward worthwhile activities of various kinds, depending on his own nature.

This is a time in the developing child's life when his energies can with equal ease rise or sink in the scale of spiritual "lightness" and "heaviness." Without proper guidance, he may become contractive in his feelings, consequently dwelling too much on himself and his own problems, if he is naturally introverted; or entering into intense ego-competition with others, if his nature is outgoing. Properly guided, however, these years can develop into a wonderful period of active and practical idealism.

Those adults are mistaken who write off the teen-age years as a period to be merely survived—if possible! I even wonder whether much of the problem that children face during their teens is not due to the powerfully negative image projected onto them at this time of their lives by adults.

It is painfully evident, especially to parents, that adolescents are no longer the sweet, innocent, trusting, and—dare I say it?—cuddly children of yesterday. Infants—indeed, the very young of all species—have something beautiful that, to everyone's regret, they lose as they grow up. It isn't merely their small size. A baby elephant, after all, is already larger than an adult human being. Rather, it is the trust we see in their eyes. They haven't yet learned to suspect the intentions of an indifferent or hostile world.

Jim Corbett, the famous tiger hunter, did his favorite hunting with a camera. One day he was lying in a tree on a platform, called in India a *machan*. He had his camera ready, when he saw a grown Bengal tiger stalk a kid goat. At some point during the tiger's advance the kid heard him and turned around. Observing this unknown but enormous creature, it tottered over trustingly and began to sniff at him with curiosity.

Well, how could the tiger finish his attack? On the other hand, what was he to do? He rose from his crouch and, to save face, allowed the kid to sniff at him a few moments longer. Then, with great dignity, he turned away and walked off into the jungle.

The sweet innocence of infancy is lost not only in human beings, but in all animals, when they reach the age of sexual maturity. Parents—mothers, especially—cannot avoid a certain sadness in the loss. (I'll never forget my mother's response when, at the age of forty-five, I gave her a birthday card that showed a big bruiser of a man with a large, stubble chin chewing on a cigar that stuck out of the side of his mouth. He was dressed in a little sailor suit with short pants, and held a balloon in one hand. The message below the picture read, "Happy birthday, Mommy, from your little boy."

How delightedly my mother laughed! It so aptly expressed her own secret attitude toward us boys.)

Nevertheless, adolescence inevitably brings on a change. The thing is to do one's best to make it a *good* change. Of vital assistance in this regard is to project positive expectations onto the teenager.

Proper training during the first twelve years, and proper reference, later, to the values learned during those years, will be a great aid in turning this third six-year period into a time of real development toward maturity.

The Thoughtful Years

At eighteen, finally, the child is ready to give full attention to developing his intellect. Much more than a time of learning to reason cleverly—a skill that he may indeed have already shown by the age of three!—this is a time for learning to reason *clearly*—that is to say, with discernment and discrimination.

At twenty-four, there may not be any obvious biological change to suggest that, the six years of intellectual unfoldment having ended, the young adult is ready at last to enter the world of grownups. In fact, college usually lasts only four years, after which a young man or woman is expected to get out there and shoulder adult responsibility with everyone else. From my own observation of young people at that age, however, I am inclined to recommend that they not be forced out of the learning mode until they actually turn twenty-four.

Some children from very early in life may be more naturally inclined toward feeling, will, or reason. An intellectually gifted child, for example, may reveal the gift of reasoning almost with the first words he utters. And an infant of naturally strong will may make his wishes unmistakenly known in the cradle. There have been many brilliant people, however, even geniuses, who never achieved the equilibrium of true maturity in their lives, being perhaps physically inept, or emotionally immature, or whimsical in the exertion of will power, or even, in their very brilliance, blind to many fundamental realities. Such people are, for these very reasons, not completely successful as human beings. Again, there have been many people of great will power who yet lacked the ability to feel sensitively. Examples of similar imbalances are to be found in all the four stages of maturity.

Whatever the child's intrinsic ability, then, it would be wise not to deprive him of his natural development through these four sequential stages. While giving recognition to his intellectual needs and gifts, for example, remember also that a six-year-old is still a child, and that other aspects of his nature must be brought to maturity if he is ever to live a full, and fulfilled, life. The four stages should each be given its due importance during the growing years.

The Adult Years

Adults, too, have their twenty-four-year cycles of development toward true maturity. Education doesn't end with graduation from formal schooling. The first twenty-four are meant to ground them in the essential tools, but after that much work remains.

The next twenty-four years, more or less until the age of forty-eight, are for giving back to the world in a material sense what the person has received during his growing years.

The twenty-four after that are for withdrawing to some extent from the battlefield, while coaching the younger ones in the knowledge he has gained in life's struggle.

The remainder of his life, from more or less the age of seventy-two, is for concentrating more on sharing his acquired wisdom with others, as opposed to sharing his practical knowledge (which may in fact, by this time, be growing obsolete anyway). This is also a period during which a person will seek to prepare himself, if he is wise, for passing life's "final exam." It is a time, ideally, for meditation and contemplation of the eternal verities.

These cycles of adulthood might easily make the subject of a book. An elaborate treatment of them would be out of place, however, in this book, dedicated as it is to childhood education.

Chapter 16

The Foundation Years

The first six—generally, the pre-school—years of a child's life are the most important for establishing a direction that will last him a lifetime. Care should be taken to inculcate in him wholesome habits, tastes, and attitudes. It is during these years especially that the adage holds: "As the twig inclineth, so doth the tree grow."

For this reason also it might be well for the child to be enrolled in some kind of pre-school, to learn along with others, and under a teacher trained in these methods of instruction, of which few parents have any actual experience.

During the first six years, as we have seen, a child can learn best through the medium of his body, and by developing his awareness through the five senses.

Muscular and motor control is, perhaps, the most difficult thing to learn in the beginning. The little child needs to be made progressively aware of his body, of its limitations and its strengths. While developing this awareness, he can learn other things better if he is invited to act them out, instead of having them explained to him merely.

As I pointed out earlier, children naturally enjoy playing games of "Let's Pretend." Acting out stories, working out situations by having Jimmy stand here, Mary over there, and you too somewhere, as part of the story, with everyone actually going through the parts, will make a much deeper impression on their minds than simply talking things out with them.

I am not much in favor of carrying this thought to its logical conclusion of walking the child through *every* lesson, or having him always act it out with his body. One might easily, for instance, in the present context, leap to the idea of teaching numbers or the alphabet by drawing great designs on the floor, and having the child trace out those outlines by walking along them. Never in later life is he likely to have to pace these things out with his feet. Most probably, he will always work with them with his hands and fingers.

A system taught me when I was a child was, I think, more realistic. It made use of the body also, moreover—of the hands, in this case, rather than the feet. We were given letters and numbers printed large on a page, and textured like sand paper. Then we were asked to trace these shapes with our forefingers.

Another excellent way of teaching children by using their bodies is to involve them in simple dramatic presentations, with a minimum of words and a maximum of action. A suggestion: Let them have fun, even if it disturbs the plot!

Dance movement can be an excellent means both of teaching bodily coordination and of developing spiritually "light" mental attitudes.

Any upward movement of the arms, head, or torso can be used to suggest a rising awareness, and any downward movement to suggest heaviness of mind and feeling. Children might be encouraged, while dancing, to concentrate more on their shoulders, arms, and hands, and correspondingly less on their lower limbs.

The major focus of many dances is on the lower part of the body: the hips, legs, and feet. In normal life, these parts receive considerably less attention; their role is generally a supporting one. Normally, when people express their feelings or ideas physically, isn't it natural for them to use their arms and hands? It seems therefore right, in the consciousness-raising dances to which I refer, to keep the lower limbs more in their naturally supportive role.

I am not suggesting always choreographing children's dances. Spontaneity should be encouraged as much as possible. Why not, rather, give names to various dance movements that will of themselves suggest the kinds of gestures intended?

One dance, for example, might be called, "Scattering Flowers."

Another, "Sharing the Sunlight."

Another, "Making Rainbows."

Still another, "Waking the World."

"Trees Dancing" could make a delightful and unusual dance. So also could "Offering," and "Catching the Rain."

One dance, in which the legs and feet would receive full and enthusiastic play, might be called, "Stalking an Opportunity."

An important point to remember, I think, is not to suggest dances that the child might come to ridicule later on in life. For by such ridicule a prejudice might develop around the whole system. "Birds in Flight," for example, might be a perfectly good dance exercise, provided the birds visualized were large, soaring birds with broad wing spans and calm beauty. If, however, the children were to set themselves flapping and hopping about like little sparrows, they might have a good laugh at the time, but in later years they might remember the scene in all its absurdity, and, embarrassed at the memory, tell their friends, "All I remember is, we used to hop madly about like a bunch of silly birds!" Impressions stored up at a young age often linger on in the memory as caricatures.

One means of using physical movement to impart important lessons along with body coordination is through painting and drawing in color. An excellent practice would be to get a class, in cooperation with the teacher, to paint story scenes together, each child designing a different part of the scene.

Colors are important to most children. Children can also be made aware of the effect of different colors, and of different shades of color, on their feelings. They can be helped to see, for example, how they themselves may choose to use a preponderance of red when they feel angry or resentful, and blue when they feel peaceful and calm.

The purer the color, the "lighter" and more expanded, usually, its influence on the mind. A teacher might get children to look into the prism of lights in a crystal; even to imagine themselves moving about in a magical world of rainbow hues. At this point, the teacher might invent a story, perhaps of a child entering such a world and having wonderful adventures with beings and places of radiant light.

A game the children might also play could be called, "Cheering Up the Colors." For this game, the children could be invited to take dull, unhappy hues and make them pure, bright, and happy.

Music and sound are important to a child's development. But what kind of music, and what kinds of sound?

Much popular modern music has been demonstrated repeatedly to have a harmful effect on the nervous system. The heavy beat of rock music is so deleterious that even plants, during experiment, have sent out tendrils in an opposite direction from the loudspeakers that were blaring it forth, as though desperate to escape their planter boxes! On the other hand, when classical music was played continuously, the plants reversed their direction and actually sent out tendrils to embrace the loudspeakers!

One can't expect to change a whole culture (if culture is, in this case, the *mot juste*), but one can at least speak one's mind to anyone who is willing to listen.

The beat of much popular modern music is, in fact, contractive and heavy. It is ego-affirming, not ego-expansive. It takes the mind downward. There are few sights stranger or more incongruous, or less attractive, than a little child stamping its feet and writhing about to the violent music of a rock band. Naturally, children find an appeal in this kind of music, for it affirms their egos. The ego is already their natural center. But is this affirmation wholesome for their development toward maturity? If the thesis of this book is correct, then the answer must be, Surely not.

Much of popular modern music works directly contrary to any serious attempt to help children in their development towards maturity.

Music plays a vitally important role in life, and should therefore play such a role also in education. By rhythm and melody, the mind can be inspired with devotion, or fired to risk life in battle; softened to sentiments of kindness and love; tickled to laughter; soothed to relaxation; or kindled to anger and violence. One popular song years ago, called "Gloomy Sunday," was eventually banned from the airwaves because too many people, after listening to it repeatedly, committed suicide.

It has even been found that lessons learned against a background of baroque music, with its approximately sixty beats to the minute, register more deeply in the mind.

A delightful song in the movie "The Sound of Music" has the von Trappe children singing a melody while naming the notes, thus: "Sol do la fa mi do re, sol do la ti do re do." I've never heard of children actually being taught to sing this way in school, but it seems an excellent idea. For by thus naming the notes, they should, I imagine, quickly learn them well enough to recognize them in any sequence.

Instead of the usual sequence, however—"Do re mi fa sol la ti (or si) do"—children might enjoy it more if they named familiar things, and didn't merely utter meaningless sounds. "Sol," moreover—the fifth note of the scale as it is normally sung—is a slightly clumsy syllable when followed by certain of the other notes: "sol re," for example, or "sol mi."

What about other sounds for the major scale: "Day, lark, rose, tree, moon, night, sea, day"? I propose these partly because they flow well together in any sequence, and partly because they are poetic and can bring the notes more to life. In-between notes (the sharps in the C scale) might be named as they are here in parenthesis: "Day (break), lark (song), rose, tree (leaf), moon (ray), night (cloud), sea, day." These incidentals would, of course, help only those children who were already somewhat grounded in music.

Thus, the above melody would be sung: "Moon day night tree rose day lark, Moon day night sea day lark day."

Games of imagination might be played with individual notes, or with groups of notes.

Nature will provide the teacher with endless opportunities for expanding children's awareness. A game with great possibilities might be called, "Tuning In to Nature." For this game, take the children out of doors, and—as an example—stand them around a tree, then ask them to suggest what they might learn from the tree. They may answer, Strength, Firmness of purpose, and so on. Ask them, then, to tune in to the tree and try to draw these qualities from it.

A fascinating book on this subject is Joseph Cornell's *Sharing Nature with Children.**

An excellent practice, too, would be for the children to tune in to one another: to strive to *feel* qualities in their schoolmates that could be helpful to themselves. They could even be encouraged to bless one another. In these ways, their natural childish tendency to scoff at their peers could be transformed into a tendency to be charitable.

They might also be invited to make garlands of wild flowers and garland one another, as well as the teacher and, perhaps, the children and teachers in other classrooms.

Thus, in all ways the children may be educated to respond to life with the best that is in them, and each one to develop to his own highest potential.

---

* Dawn Publications, Nevada City, California.

Chapter 17

The Feeling Years

Many of the techniques and principles suggested in the last chapter can be carried through effectively into the later school years. The first three grades, especially, can be used to develop and refine everything this book has suggested for the pre-school years.

Moreover, it isn't at all the case that, with the end of those first six years, the method of teaching through body awareness ought to be abandoned. In various ways, in fact, teaching through body movement should be continued throughout the years of formal education; indeed, it will prove useful throughout life. For every mental attitude has its counterpart in physical positions and gestures. The body and the mind are forever both interrelated and interactive.

What we must do, then, is not abandon one emphasis for another as the child grows from one six-year stage to the next. The first stage, rather, should serve as a foundation upon which the second stage of the building can be erected. The second stage, in its turn, makes possible the construction of the third, and the third, of the fourth. Each progressive stage only raises the building higher; it doesn't call for a shift elsewhere and the construction of a new building.

The first three years of grade school, especially, will call for a fuller development of the techniques suggested for the pre-school years, with the addition of a greater emphasis on emotional development and inspiration.

During the second three years of grade school, the teaching can become less concrete and more abstract. The child's mind will now be more adept at handling concepts *as* concepts, rather than as images that must be acted out physically in order to be truly grasped.

The emphasis throughout this second six-year phase of education should be on teaching through the feelings and the emotions, and particularly on developing the finer feelings. For it is during these years that the child can begin to direct his emotions constructively, instead of letting them rule him.

Many thinking people, raised in what is, relatively speaking, an emotionally arid society, consider it quite enough merely to be able once again to *express* emotion. "Get in touch with your feelings" was the advice making the rounds a few years ago. (And never mind if those feelings happen to be destructive.) Partly, the idea was that, by recognizing negative emotions, one would be able to change them. And partly it was that, by expressing them, one would be able to release them.

Major changes in people's lives, however, have not been found to result from this system. Simple mental recognition of a problem hasn't provided the requisite energy for banishing the problem. Worse still, as we've seen earlier in this book, *too much* mental recognition, and the intellectual conceptualization that such recognition entails, may actually rob people of the energy they need for practical action.

Simply to give vent to a poisonous emotion by no means effects a permanent cure. The very technique is interestingly reminiscent of the practice of bloodletting by leeches in the days of earlier, less sophisticated medicine. Granted, one may feel a temporary release after screaming with impotent exaggeration such maledictions as, "I want to kill my father!" or weeping with helpless abandon for all the sorrows one has ever endured. Such release, however, if indeed it *is* release and not merely exhaustion, is short-lived. For there is always, in such emotional "bloodletting," the thought, "*I* want," or "*I* grieve"—that sturdy thread by which the supposedly exorcised feeling remains firmly fettered to the ego.

It is difficult enough even for adults to escape their emotional problems by merely becoming aware of them. But adults have at least other frames of reference by which to reduce any given emotion to its relative insignificance. Children have no such broadened perspective. They suffer from what might be termed emotional tunnel vision. Any emotion presently endured by a child becomes for him an all-absorbing, wholly present reality.

Simply put, children have no need to "get in touch with their feelings"; they already live in those feelings. They have no need to affirm their negative emotions; any such affirmation will only strengthen those emotions. Nothing can be gained by forcing them to suppress their emotions. What they need, rather, is to learn how to *channel* those emotions positively.

One classic example of society's effort to suppress feelings, rather than rechannel them, is the common admonition to a sobbing little boy, "Come on, Johnny, boys don't cry." What's wrong with crying, for heaven's sake? *Of course* a boy should feel free to cry if he feels like it. Strength doesn't lie in the suppression of tears. It lies in the ability to *redirect* negative feelings.

It *is* weakness, on the other hand, not to be able to redirect them. And it feeds that weakness to show a boy (or a girl, for that matter) too much pity. Show enough concern to let him or her know that you understand and empathize. But then, instead of merely trying to get the child to stop crying, try to get him to redirect this grief in a new and positive direction—preferably one relevant to what he has been crying about, rather than urging him simply to "Come on outside and play."

We examined in some detail, earlier, the importance of helping a child to raise his consciousness, and—almost synonymously—to expand it. He could be taught to do both, quite literally, as a means of redirecting his feelings.

First, you might get him to sit up straight, to look upward, and take a few deep breaths.

Next, get him to think more expansively: for instance, to consider the situation from the other's point of view (if his feelings have been hurt); or to see whatever happened as small or temporary, relative to his own broader realities; to be fair-minded; to look upon whoever hurt him as needing his help and understanding.

It is important not to belittle his feelings. This is what creates harmful repressions. Try simply, instead, to get him to see those feelings in a broader perspective. Thus you may reduce the importance in his own eyes of his negative feelings.

It will be helpful also to teach your pupils the ability to abstract every feeling, and even their own personality traits, from their total reality and from that of others—to put it more simply, to help them to look at their own feelings objectively. They can be helped to see that moodiness, for example, is not an essential characteristic of even the moodiest child; that we are not our personalities, but something far deeper which watches consciously from within. Thus you can help them to understand that every undesirable trait can be changed without, in the process, losing something of themselves.

It will help the child very much to realize that moodiness or anger doesn't define him, himself, as a person of moods or anger. By distancing himself a little from his emotions, he will find it easier to transform them into positive feelings.

One way to teach this mental abstraction might be, first, through simple arithmetic addition and subtraction. Take two apples, for example; then two more apples. Together they make four apples. Do the same thing with oranges. The result in each case is the same. The essential thing, then, in this addition is not the objects used, whether apples or oranges. It is the two-ness of them, which becomes, with addition, a four-ness. Both qualities have nothing to do with whether they are apples or oranges.

The same principle might then be applied to such abstractions as lightness and heaviness. Cotton, for example, as it grows on the plant is light and fluffy. In a ship's sail, however, it is compressed and heavy. Lightness or heaviness too, then, are abstractions. An object may manifest one or the other of these properties without being defined by either of them. Iron, for example, will sink in water. In this context it is heavy. But it will float in mercury, which fact makes it, in this new context, light.

Study the lives of great people. Show how they *developed* heroism, courage, kindness; they weren't necessarily born with these qualities. Show also how, by repeated acts of selfishness, people can *become* mean, spiritually "heavy," and miserable.

In this way, the child can be taught to believe in his own ability to change, and also to separate others, in his own mind, from their faults: "Hate the sin," as the saying goes, "but not the sinner."

To help him to overcome a tendency to judge others, it may be emphasized to him that a person develops in himself any trait on which he concentrates, even if he looks for it in other people. Thus, if there is any quality that he dislikes in another child, and if he mentally judges the child for possessing that quality, he will attract that same quality to himself. He should try therefore to help others, and not condemn them, if only because by so doing he will help himself.

It may also be possible to help him see that he never hates qualities in others if there isn't at least a suggestion of that quality in himself. Thus, he can turn impetuous judgment of others into a tool for self-understanding and self-transformation.

Stories of great people are always inspiring. During this second six-year period of life, such stories have a particularly strong impact and can help to mold the child's entire future development.

It is a pity to offer children nothing but entertainment, in the form of frivolous and meaningless tales, when human history has produced an abundance of worthwhile fables, allegories, and true episodes that make wonderful reading, and that are by turns amusing, witty, inspiring, and beautiful—everything, in short, that any story for children may aspire to be.

The six-to-nine years are also an excellent time for learning something about the arts: painting, sculpture, music; and for getting a taste of the sheer romance of the great scientific discoveries.

Children in this age-bracket can be taught the difference between the right and wrong use of their physical senses. The eyes, for example, should be trained to see truth and beauty, not ugliness and falsehood. The ears should be trained to concentrate on absorbing goodness; on hearing kind words, beautiful sounds, and beautiful music—and not on absorbing depressing news, unkind words, negative judgments about others, ugly sounds, and ugly music. To repeat, we become whatever we concentrate on.

The tongue should be trained, similarly, to enjoy wholesome food, and to speak kind words. The sense of touch should be disciplined to become a servant of the will, and instantly obedient to it, instead of being allowed to revel in physical sensations to the extent of enslaving one. The sense of smell should be sensitized to the fragrance of fresh flowers, herbs, and forest scents, and taught to avoid, or (when necessary) to rise above stale smells like exhaust fumes, cigarette smoke, and air-conditioned rooms.

The imagination should be trained also. A well developed and healthy imagination is the spring from which flows the creativity of genius. Visualizations can be offered to children as a means of stimulating their imagination.

For instance, tell them: "Imagine yourself living in a forest. What is the forest like? Are you afraid, or are you happy there? Build yourself a home in the forest. What kind of a home would you like to build? Is it in a clearing, or in the deep woods?

"Think of the forest animals. Are they your friends? or are you afraid of any of them? If so, why?

"See yourself walking along a forest path. Whom do you meet there? Is it an animal, or a human being? If it's a human being, does that person smile when he or she sees you? Have you done something to make him or her smile? If not, is there something you can do to make this friend smile?

"Imagine a pond in the forest. In the middle of this pond, there is a small island, and on the island a cup rests on a marble pedestal. What does the cup look like? Describe it. Does it contain something good to drink? What is that drink?

"Think of the cup as containing a wonderful, clear amber liquid, bubbling with energy and happiness. Drink it. Suddenly: Look! Everything in the forest is becoming cheerful, peaceful, and beautiful—full of sunshine and hope.

"Call to your friends, whoever they may be: children, grown-ups, or animals. Ask them to come and enjoy this magical drink with you. Now, walk with them through the magical forest."

Countless similar exercises might be used to stimulate the children's imaginations. These exercises can become themes for whatever paintings they create, subsequently.

Children need to learn to *practice* cheerfulness—to be helped, in other words, to see that cheerfulness isn't only a mood that one feels when things go right; that one must work consciously at *being* cheerful, no matter what the surrounding circumstances.

Affirmations should become, during this second six-year stage of life, an important part of the child's daily routine, especially affirmations repeated with the movements suggested in Chapter 9.

Where music is concerned, during the first six years many children will be more adept at appreciating it than at creating it. By the second six years, however, many of them should be ready for some sort of creativity. Those with sufficient talent could be invited to sing choral pieces together, to practice the Suzuki method of playing the violin, and in other ways to develop their musical sense.

Those with a talent for dancing could be encouraged to interpret music through dance movements, once they've been shown how different kinds of music correspond to different feelings in the heart.

Wholesome habits should be inculcated: cleanliness, a sense of neatness and order, even-mindedness, contentment, truthfulness, a cooperative spirit, servicefulness, responsibility, and respect toward others (especially toward one's elders).

Exercises can be used to help the child to become centered in himself—not self-centered, which is something altogether different, but restful and relaxed at his own inner center. Certain yoga postures are excellent for developing this awareness, with their gentle stretches left, right, forward, and back, returning after every stretch to a position of rest in the middle.

Concentration, too, is vitally important in the child's development. Concentration is commonly associated with knitted eyebrows and mental tension, but true concentration has nothing to do with strain. Rather, it means, simply, *absorption* in a thought or a perception, or in the search for a solution. Such an ability is vital for success of all kinds in life.

Get the children to practice concentration daily for brief periods, until it becomes habitual with them. There are many effective techniques for developing concentration. Remind the children, for example, how naturally they concentrate on anything, if it really interests them—a good movie, for instance, or an interesting story. Suggest that they look at an unmoving object with similar interest: a flower, a candle, the lights in a crystal. Remind them that they can create interest within, and project it outwardly; that they needn't wait for interest to be awakened in them by objective stimulation; and that this interest, when focused, is all that is meant by concentration.

The best feelings are those which lift one in aspiration toward higher realities. In this soaring aspiration, lesser qualities become almost effortlessly uplifted also, even as a tendency to offer petty criticism can be transcended by a willingness to give one's life for others. Not to teach children to feel devotion to God and to high ideals seems to me the greatest disservice one can render them. It is like producing a body without a head, or a limousine with only a one-horse-power engine.

I am reminded here of an encounter that I had, years ago, with a young man who was aggressively atheistic. Though I tried to broaden his understanding by suggesting that God is a universal concept, I got nowhere.

Later that evening I offered him and a few others rides to their various destinations. A sixteen-year-old girl in the car made the statement, apropos of nothing, "I don't believe in love."

After I'd let her off at her home, the self-styled atheist turned to me in amazement. "Can you imagine that?" he exclaimed: "Not believing in love!"

Chuckling I replied, "And you call yourself an atheist?"

Chapter 18

The Willful Years

The immediate inspiration for this book was a dream I had, in which a group of aggressive teenage boys surrounded me arrogantly. I wasn't apprehensive, but I do recall experiencing a deep concern for them.

As we walked up a street, talking together—they, hunching along in the self-conscious manner of many teenagers—I remarked, "Doesn't it seem that life ought to offer us something really worth living for? Surely kindness and friendship are worth more than being considered important? And isn't happiness something worth striving for, rather than something to reject as impossible?"

"That's right!" they exclaimed a little sadly. "It's what we all want."

And I felt their own deep intrinsic worth, their sense of innocence betrayed by an upbringing that had stripped them of everything in which they might have had faith.

The problems of modern education are evident during all the four stages, but they become glaringly so during the teenage years—the third stage.

It is, as I've already stated, during this six-year stage that the child feels a special need to test his will power. It isn't that he won't test it sooner, any more than a child during its first six years, though focused on developing bodily awareness, doesn't express its emotions. (As I remarked earlier, it is probable during those first years that he'll seem to be expressing little else!)

A child with a naturally strong will may show will-fulness in the very cradle. Yogananda used to say that it is a mistake, though one that is often committed for the parents' convenience, to discourage willfulness. However, just as the best time for learning to control the emotions is during the second six-year stage, so also the best time for consciously developing the will power and directing it wisely is during the third stage, up to the age of eighteen.

Idealism, for example, develops naturally with only a little encouragement during the six years preceding a child's twelfth birthday. But it tends to be an idealism more sentimental than practical. With the adolescent's dawning instinct for expressing his will power, there comes the inclination to put idealism into practice. Such, at least, is the *opportunity* of adolescence. Alas, it proves all too often an opportunity either overlooked or unrecognized.

For with the onset of puberty there comes a growing preoccupation with oneself *as* a self—as an ego separate and distinct from other egos. The child's developing sexual awareness forces upon him a major redefinition of his priorities—of how he sees himself, how he relates to others, and what he expects from life.

Sexual awareness tends to pull the adolescent's energy and consciousness downward, toward spiritual "heaviness." This directional flow, coupled with his natural self-preoccupation, is contractive in effect, resulting in deep psychological pain for the child. If, moreover, his natural mental inclination is upward, this unaccustomed downward flow brings him also into a period of spiritual confusion.

With sexual awareness also, on the other hand, there comes a sense of potential inner power, of creativity, which, if not directed into right channels, may easily be diverted into destructive ones.

Should the mind, during this third stage, be brought to repudiate the idealism it held as a younger child, it may reject ideals altogether and employ all of its creative power cynically, in acts that are deliberately negative.

How can an adolescent be encouraged to keep his early idealism? Advantage may actually be taken of the changes occurring in his body and psyche with the advent of puberty.

His awakening sense of inner power can be directed toward making his ideals practical, instead of rejecting them negatively as the figment of dreams. Early dreams must now be translated into dynamic action—refined in their definition, perhaps, but not abandoned cynically.

Adolescence needs a cause—or, better still, an abundance of causes. It needs something to *do*. It is like dynamite: if exploded above the ground it may only destroy; but if placed carefully underground and exploded there, it may help in the building of roads over which cars will pass later.

Adolescence, when approached and understood rightly, is a wonderful time, rich with some of life's greatest opportunities for self-development. The important thing to understand is the youth's need for *action,* and not for mere theories.

Physical discipline is important. So also is any call to good deeds without the expectation of personal reward—the greater the self-sacrifice entailed, the better, provided, of course, that the child's welfare isn't endangered.

Self-reliance needs to be stressed in numerous ways, including camping out in the wilderness, boy scout activities, tests of personal endurance and the like.

Other tests can be given the teenager for developing his will power. If he feels a cold coming on, for example, he might try casting it out of his body by sheer will power. (This can be done quite effectively, provided the cold is caught at an early enough stage.)

He can be encouraged to test the power of positive thinking, and to see how it affects his own life, the lives of others, and objective circumstances. A positive, strong will power has been shown to be capable of influencing objective events, and above all one's own consciousness, for the better.

The teenager, so often pampered by worried adults, actually needs just the opposite from them: *challenges!* Dare him to do better than he imagines possible. But *draw* him forward, don't yank him or push him. His responses must arise out of himself; they must not be imposed upon him unnaturally by ambitious grown-ups.

What is to be done about teenagers who are already going in wrong directions? It is all very well to approach adolescence as a wonderful time of life, provided we can begin working on the adolescent right from the age of twelve. But what about the great numbers of older adolescents who have already developed strongly negative behavioral patterns? Is there any hope for them?

Indeed there is, though admittedly, in this case, the task will be more difficult. All of the above guidelines will apply. Negativity must be recognized and dealt with honestly. *Faith* in the child's potential, however, must be the underlying attitude; never accept his negative self-image.

The important thing is to realize that most children do want true values. Their negativity is symptomatic, usually, of disillusionment, because they've been deprived of faith.

Two courses of direction have the potential to transform the currently destructive atmosphere surrounding youth in society. One would be a spiritual renascence of some deep, experiential kind. This, obviously, is not something that can be produced to order. The other would be the opposite of pampering: firm, but kind, discipline.

Disciplining children without love never really works. I don't recommend a boot camp type of training, which would only undermine the good work done during the ages of six to twelve, the feeling years. But it might help for people at least to understand the value of stern discipline, lest love be equated with feeble smiles and futile remonstrances.

In the Swiss army many years ago there was a regiment that consisted of the lowest and roughest elements of society, men who categorically refused every form of discipline. They rose in the morning whenever they felt like it; showed up for drill or not, as it pleased them; talked back to their officers, and made it abundantly clear that they had nothing but contempt for a law that made it mandatory for every adult male in Switzerland to serve his time in the army. The officers were afraid of them, and didn't dare to enforce discipline on them.

Then a new colonel was placed over them. This man was not the type to put up with such nonsense. Impatient with their slovenly behavior, he decided that what they needed was severe discipline, not laxity. His fellow officers waited with bated breath for the inevitable-seeming shot in the back.

But this regiment somehow accepted the colonel's no-nonsense approach. Within a few months, they became the best-disciplined group in the entire army, and the unit with the highest esprit de corps.

I don't recommend such Spartan measures with teenagers, but as long as parents and teachers are afraid to be firm, even in much milder ways, poor discipline will be endemic in the schools, along with the many negative attitudes that result from it.

Too many adults, unfortunately, are more concerned with being loved than with loving. If they really loved, they would give the children what they really need. During adolescence, the child's will power needs to be tested and strengthened, not merely shrugged off as a test for the grown-ups.

"What If I Fail?"

One of the most sensitive areas of adolescence is the ever-present possibility of failure. This threat is, to be sure, never far absent even from the minds of many adults. But for the adolescent, the slightest gaffe, the most trivial manifestation of gaucherie on his part, assumes nightmare dimensions, and is magnified to unforgettably ludicrous proportions in the minds of his companions.

Failure must be addressed, therefore, and not shunned as too embarrassing a topic for open discussion.

In fact, failure is actually intrinsic to the ultimate achievement of success. Anyone who never fails never, by the same token, really succeeds. For success is much more a question of achievement than of accomplishment. What is the difference? If Superman can outrun an express train, that is an accomplishment, certainly, but it isn't an achievement, for there was nothing he needed to overcome by running so fast. We all know that if the occasion demanded it he could run twice, or even ten times, as fast. Accomplishment, without the possibility of failure, is very different from achievement in the face of great obstacles. Failure, then, is an instrument of learning. Every failure accepted, understood, then placed resolutely behind one can be an important stepping stone to higher achievement.

It is never wise, then, to say, "I've failed." The courage that leads to achievement says, "I haven't yet succeeded." The repeated thought of failure acts as a negative affirmation; if it doesn't actually attract failure, it creates the conditions for failure by slowly weakening the will power. But the repeated thought of success, even in the face of repeated failures, is an affirmation that *must,* eventually, produce the achievement one desires.

The adolescent must be helped to see that anyone who never fails has failed already, in a sense. A career unblemished by failures is a story of minimal courage, perhaps even of cowardice. It is a story of one who, having never dared, has never developed as a human being. Great success is the fruit of great daring. No matter how many times a person fails, victory is assured him if, after every defeat, he gets up and tries again. Indeed, if his courage never flags, he can squeeze victory of a sort even from crushing defeat.

As Paramhansa Yogananda used to say, of the spiritual search: "A saint is a sinner who never gave up!"

Self-Control

The adolescent should be taught the importance of disciplining himself, and not merely receiving discipline outwardly. He may find it helpful, for example, to fast occasionally, or to go for periods of time without some favorite food; to do things against which his desire for comfort rebels; to do things for others with the deliberate purpose of overcoming selfishness in himself.

Servicefulness is a wonderful quality, and one too little appreciated in this age of aggressive self-affirmation. There is joy in the expansive consciousness of forgetting oneself in the thought of a larger good.

Affirmations, too, some of which have been suggested already, can be an excellent tool of self-discipline and self-transformation.

A good book on behavior is Dale Carnegie's *How to Win Friends and Influence People.* The title, in the present social atmosphere, may sound as if the book is about how to manipulate others, but it is in fact an invaluable guide for anyone wanting to learn how to behave sensitively toward other people. An excellent maxim of Carnegie's is, "Act enthusiastic, and you'll *be* enthusiastic!"

Lack of enthusiasm is, in fact, one of the pitfalls of adolescence. An excellent way of climbing out of this pit is to express enthusiasm vigorously in both word and action, even if one feels no enthusiasm in his heart. The greater the outward expression of will, the greater will be the flow of energy to succeed at anything one sets out to accomplish.

Young people of spiritually "light" specific gravity often find themselves at a disadvantage during their adolescent years owing to the aggressive emphasis placed on the ego by their peers. To many youngsters at that age, the ego seems all-important—a thing to be affirmed constantly, and thrust upon others as though challenging them to rival oneself in importance. Often—so it seems at that age—the greater the ego, the more powerful, magnetic, and successful the person. Hence the popularity of football heroes, and, all too frequently, the comparative obscurity of idealists.

Only later in life may the thought arise in the mind that all of us are part of a much greater reality, and that attunement with that reality is important for the accomplishment of all the really great things in life. Great scientists, for example, have never boasted to the universe, "You'll do as *I* say!" They have said humbly, rather, "Help me to understand what it is *you* are trying to teach me."

Friends of mine visited California some years ago. During their visit I took them to Disneyland, where, for one of the rides, we hired little boats big enough to accommodate two persons each.

Each boat had what looked like a steering wheel, but was in fact a dummy. Most of us soon discovered that no matter how we turned the wheels, the boat continued along its own course, which was determined by tracks under water.

At a certain point, my boat-partner and I saw a couple in their party pass near us by another channel. We hailed them, and the man's wife tried to get him to call out a greeting.

"Don't interrupt me," he cried, tensely. "Can't you see, if I'm not careful we'll hit those rocks ahead of us!"

What a laugh his family all had later on, at his expense!

And how similar is the case of many people who imagine that, in all things, it is they themselves who are the doers. They fail to realize that countless things in life simply can't be controlled, and had best be simply understood, accepted, and adjusted to.

The lesson of adolescence, ultimately, should be to strengthen not the ego, but the will, as a stepping stone towards true maturity. This stepping stone should be viewed with humility, as but one of many, by crossing all of which the adolescent will be able not only to understand, but to feel himself part of, the universal reality that surrounds him.

Chapter 19

The Thoughtful Years

When young people reach the age of eighteen, they suddenly—or so it may seem—start to sit about in little groups discussing politics, philosophy, religion, the meaning of life, and other abstract subjects—or, alternatively, business trends, or the latest scientific theories and discoveries. This frequently abrupt change in behavior is not due only to a change in the subject matter of their classes. More probably, those very changes in the methods of teaching are due to the perceived need to adjust the subject matter to the changes occurring in the students' very attitudes.

During these thoughtful years, the young person is likely to begin to appreciate the truth of those famous words of the poet Bulwer-Lytton: "The pen is mightier than the sword." For with the unfolding of the intellect, youth enters the fascinating world of ideas and discovers there a power greater than material force.

The important thing during this stage is, as we have seen earlier, to teach young people to reason clearly, and not merely cleverly. For the intellect can be used with almost equal skill to clarify situations as to obscure them; to find positive, helpful solutions to problems as to block every hint of a worthwhile solution. The "heavier" the individual's consciousness, the greater the likelihood that he will tend toward the misuse of reason. Refined feelings alone, ultimately, can guide the reasoning faculty correctly.

Reason is a tool, merely: a path, not a goal. The student should be taught to use it honestly, lest, like a power tool in the hands of an unskilled carpenter, it slip and injure him.

The truth simply *exists*. It cannot be created; it cannot be distorted; it cannot be denied. One may play with it as shrewdly as one likes; one may put on a superb show and convince many people: Truth always wins in the end. Lies, moreover, sooner or later, are always discredited.

The student needs to be convinced of this truth by every means possible. For it is unalterable. Only by accepting it can he be certain of avoiding the temptation to which many have succumbed, to use reason's power in seeming justification of wrong ends.

How many times in history has a person, or an entire nation, insisted on a wrong course of action, and offered what seemed at the time the most logical support for their decision. Anyone believing differently was in many cases branded a heretic or a traitor.

And so the kings of Europe, encouraged by the Church, raised great armies to go off and fight in useless crusades. Priests were tortured and killed in God's name on behalf of the so-called "holy" Inquisition. Thousands invested confidently in such financial fantasies as the "South Sea Bubble" and Holland's "Tulip Mania." A whole nation enthusiastically endorsed the Nazi myth of "Aryan supremacy." And communists everywhere have subscribed to the typical partisan's definition of justice: "Truth is anything that advances the communist cause, regardless of the immediate consequences."

All who have ever tried to mold truth to their own liking have failed ingloriously in the end, no matter how many people they have succeeded in converting to their ideas for a time.

Truth alone wins, in the end.

In learning to reason wisely, the student should have emphasized to him the importance of being always willing to re-evaluate his first principles. His commitment should be not to any idea about truth, nor to any mere definition of it, *but to truth itself.*

Thus, the student should be encouraged to develop a quality that is fundamental to clear insight: the willingness at once, and without the slightest attachment to any previous opinion, to change his mind, when confronted with facts that prove his opinion to have been mistaken.

Here is a suggested classroom exercise:

Get the class fully, even emotionally, committed to an idea or to a course of action. Then give them irrefutable proof that that idea or action is, after all, erroneous.

Get them into the habit of changing mental directions, when necessary, at a moment's notice; of always keeping the needle of their mind's compass pointed toward the truth, and never toward any personal bias, no matter how attractive that bias in their own eyes.

Few scientists, even, are capable of divorcing reason from their desires so completely. The ability to do so must be classed as one of the ego's real triumphs in its long journey toward maturity. But although we may expect few students, therefore, to be free enough in their mental processes to reason with perfect clarity, no effort should be spared to make them aware of the advantages of such reasoning.

Take some—take *any*—belief that is universally held: the more emotional the students' commitment to it, the better. Many professors do something like this already. They'll take democracy, for example, and reinforce the students' commitment to democracy with the usual arguments in democracy's favor. Then they'll point out the flaws in this system of government—not, if they are wise, from a wish to undermine the students' faith in it, but simply to help them to base their faith on reasons that are held honestly, and not on emotionally sustained, a priori assumptions.

A similar exercise: Get the students emotionally committed to some *cause célèbre,* perhaps some campus issue, or perhaps—to play it safe!—something that was a hot issue several centuries ago. And then see if they can be made to listen fairly to the arguments of the other side.

Again, this exercise: Teach them to *listen* to opposing points of view on different issues—to hear other people out with respect, and not with emotion; to appreciate other ways of reasoning than their own. Show them that it isn't enough in any meaningful discussion to convince oneself; that the way to convince others is to try to understand their point of view, to accept the truth whatever it may turn out to be, and to answer others' arguments in *their* terms, as much as possible, rather than one's own.

Students need to learn that the only way to reason clearly is to *reason without attachment*. The person of clear intellect, in his willingness to accept the truth of a situation whatever it may be, finds himself able also to respect the right of others to hold divergent opinions, no matter how patently fallacious, realizing as he does so that opinions (including his own) count for very little anyway: It is truth alone that matters.

Non-attachment is necessary to the quest for truth in any matter. The important thing is to remain non-attached, but not indifferent. This "passionate dispassion" can be achieved by heartfelt dedication to the truth itself.

How, then, to develop non-attachment? It can be developed by always separating, mentally, what *is* from what merely seems to be.

Let's take a simple example: an imaginary advertisement for an even more fanciful beverage, "Muddies." The advertisement depicts a crowd of young people laughing happily as they imbibe this deadly brew. Obviously, the advertiser is trying to suggest that these people's happiness is due entirely to the fact that they are drinking "Muddies." Underlying that message is the suggestion that drinking "Muddies" is "in," and will make you acceptable to the "in" crowd: that "muddies" is, to coin a phrase, a happiness-compatible drink.

In fact, the likelihood is that people drink "Muddies" quite as frequently when they feel steeped in a state of solitary gloom. No drink, certainly, ever *produces* happiness. For happiness rises from within; it is self-generated. It is only subsequently that we project a thought of happiness onto external things and circumstances. Everything, including even—let's face the deplorable fact—"Muddies," is always neutral in its effect. It is neither positive nor negative, until we so define it in our own minds.

Consider even a circumstance that would normally be labeled negative: physical pain. Sufficient mental detachment can either minimize the pain, or dismiss it altogether.

Here's how the process works: There is the sensation itself, which, though one would rather it weren't there, is itself basically neutral. Then there is our mental definition of it as painful. Further, there is our emotional reaction: "I don't *like* this painful sensation!"

Mentally detach yourself from your emotional reaction. Think of the experience as a sensation, simply. Refuse to define it in your mind as painful, or even unpleasant.

Next, tell yourself that, since it is only a sensation, it can be defined in various ways, and not only as painful. The definition you give it, remember, will be your own reactive projection onto the sensation. Try, then, to define it as merely interesting, or noisy, or as giving you an opportunity to practice concentration, but not as something you want to reject.

Next, try not defining the sensation at all. Forget about it, and think about something else. I've tried doing so in the dentist's chair, and have actually been able to work out problems in the composition of music, or in the writing of a book. Absorbed in such questions as the right chord sequence for a musical passage, I hardly noticed what the dentist was doing.

One method for developing clear reasoning is the deliberate, though playful, practice of sophistry. Students may be invited to compete in thinking up arguments to support some stand which they know very well to be absurd. They can have a lot of fun in the process, and will be helped to recognize specious reasoning, when confronted with it in real situations.

Take this example: the comic song from the musical "Oklahoma!" in which the young ingenue sings, "I'm Just a Girl Who Can't Say No." To justify flirting she sings, "Whatcha gonna do when a feller talks purdy . . . Whatcha gonna do: Spit 'n his eye?" The point is to persuade other young ladies in the audience that it is uncivil not to flirt—that a girl shows only good breeding if she acts flirtatious with as many "fellers" as possible.

Or take this argument, often advanced by thieves in defense of burglary: "People need to learn to take better care of their property."

A man I knew once slipped on the steps of a church, and broke his arm. "The moral of this story," he declared with mock solemnity afterward, "is, never go to church."

I am not a student of the history of sophistry, but I wonder whether it was devised, originally, not as a method for deluding people with fallacious arguments, but as an amusing technique for helping the philosophy students of ancient Greece to protect themselves against the pitfalls of false reasoning.

Students should be shown the difference between not only true and false reasoning, but also between truth and fact. This is an important distinction, though one not often recognized. Let me italicize the difference, to help it to stick in your mind:

A truth is in harmony with all levels of reality, whereas a fact may be relevant to only one level of reality.

For example: A person lying in bed and desperately ill may look quite as badly as he feels. It would be perfectly in consonance with the facts to tell him, "You look terrible!" This negative statement, however, might devastate the poor fellow's efforts to recuperate.

Anyone uttering such a statement might justify it with wide-eyed innocence: "But I was only speaking the truth." This self-justification, however, could only give truth a bad name! In fact, the statement, though factual, would not be true.

For truth, as I said, is in harmony with reality on all levels. It may be a fact that the invalid looks terrible, but that simple fact doesn't take into account the patient's chances, for example—with a little encouragement—of recovery; the importance to that recovery of boosting his morale; the therapeutic value of affirming good health; even the somewhat abstract philosophical argument that, on a deeper level of his being, perfection, not imperfection, is the truth.

An important aspect of reasoning correctly is to understand the difference between reason and discrimination.

A line of reasoning will be false if its premise is wrong. Often, however, reason alone is inadequate to the task of evaluating the merits of a premise. Hence, the necessity for discrimination.

Take this example: We grow up in America in the belief that freedom is an "inalienable right." For many people, this means they have the right to do anything they like. If a person plays his radio full blast at three o'clock in the morning, he may answer his neighbors' objections with the retort, "It's a free country, isn't it?" More than reason is needed to counter his false argument. That is, there must first be the feeling that his reasoning is specious. To test oneself for such a feeling, one must pull back a little, mentally, from every argument and think, "Wait a minute! Is this true?" Discrimination weighs reason against feeling in the heart to see whether the reasoning process has a good "ring" to it; whether it feels right.

Many people reason speciously. The entertainment industry, as an example, staunchly defends violent, prurient, or otherwise tasteless movies with the argument, "It's what the people want." Discrimination, however, replies, "No, it's what you want. You are conditioning people to accept, and perhaps even in time to enjoy, what you give them, but just look how often movies that are based on beautiful and noble sentiments and ideals have outsold the trash you people are putting out." Discrimination is not cold and abstract. It results when we consult our inner feelings. Calm inner feeling cuts through the twisted cleverness of sophistry and says, "This I know to be the truth."

Great scientists employ the faculty of discernment quite as often as people who deal with matters more closely touching the human condition. Without discrimination, no one would ever know which line of reasoning to follow, out of myriad choices. The great scientist would be like thousands of lesser scientists who, perhaps no less intelligent than he, lack that quality of sensing the right direction for their thinking.

This simple fact explains why so many brilliant people, even those with the highest I.Q.s, make drastic mistakes in their lives. They have the reasoning ability: What they lack is discrimination.

Discrimination is based on intuition. It is calm inner feeling, held in a state of reason, but guided from deeper levels of consciousness. Intuition is calm awareness of what feels right inwardly—literally, in the heart. It is the surest basis for making right decisions. Rationalists may—in fact, do—scoff, but intuitive discrimination is a faculty they themselves, like everyone else, use sometimes, albeit often unknowingly. It is a faculty on which great geniuses rely constantly. Without it, mankind would never have invented the wheel, nor known what to do about fire once human beings had discovered how to produce it.

For what is the alternative? If we rely on logic alone, we find ourselves entangled in so many strands of possibility that it becomes almost impossible to move. It is feeling, not logic, that tells us, "This is the right strand to follow." Nor is it a question of simplifying by random selection. Calm, intuitive feeling points again and again to the right decisions.

Discrimination can only proceed from an awareness of reality on many levels; certainly, it cannot grow in a vacuum. Here is an example of this need for broader awareness:

In a certain university a few years ago there were two groups of aspiring writers. Both groups were talented, perhaps equally so. One group consisted of women students; the other, of men. The purpose of each group was to help its members to develop their writing skills.

The men tried to accomplish this end by critiquing one another's papers. This in their eyes meant criticizing them. Any paper submitted to the group would be analyzed by the other members for its flaws.

The women, on the other hand, although analytical also, understood the additional value of offering positive suggestions.

Of the men's group, not one went on after graduation to become a professional writer. Of the women's group, several achieved fame later on as authors, editors, and reporters.

Both groups used intellectual analysis skillfully. The men, however, used it to address the only level of reality that appeared relevant to them at the time: the manuscripts. The women used it to address other levels as well: the need of each member above all to believe in herself and in her ability. Both groups may have reasoned with equal clarity, but they didn't do so with equal effectiveness.

A worthwhile exercise in the classroom would be to set up positive encounter groups.

We are familiar with the negative type of encounter group, where people sit about and tear one another to psychological shreds. The tradition is by no means new. Christian monks and nuns have made it a practice for centuries. They would (and, I suppose, still do) gather together and draw one another's attention—in "Christian charity"—to their spiritual flaws.

Far better, I believe, would be another kind of encounter group altogether: one in which the students offered one another suggestions in true charity: suggestions, for instance, for strengthening their positive qualities. In the process, each member of the group would be assisting, even unwittingly, the development of such qualities in himself.

Young people need to learn how to reason well, but also effectively—that is to say, appropriately. They must learn how to recognize when the time is right for analysis—for separating and distinguishing things and concepts from one another—and when the time has come for putting things together and making them work as a harmonious whole. The intellect must learn when to function on a level of abstraction, and when to shift to a level of encouragement and compassion.

The intellect must join feeling in discerning that there are, in fact, many levels of reality.

Maturity, as I have said, means the ability to relate appropriately to other realities than one's own. In human affairs, then, it means the ability to relate to other human realities, and not merely to the things in which human beings happen to be involved.

In the above instances, it was the people as writers who needed developing, even more than their manuscripts. The men failed because they treated one another primarily as producers of manuscripts, not as human beings. The women succeeded because, in the modern expression, they got their priorities straight.

Discrimination is the ability to perceive various levels of reality at once, and to sense which among them, in any given situation, are of primary importance.

Discrimination is impossible without humility, for it demands an understanding that truth exists already, that it cannot be created, but only perceived.

As a part of such humility, students should be taught to respect the insights of others, and above all to respect the longer rhythms and traditions of civilization: those accepted verities which, through the ages, have clarified the difference between wisdom and ignorance.

More important even than valid traditions is the possibility of fresh, but valid, discoveries. In freshness lies creativity, and in creativity lies self-expansion. A well-stated definition may help us to rise from one level of understanding to another, but no definition can serve in place of the reality it defines. The student should be encouraged to be always ready to discard old definitions in favor of new, fuller insights into reality.

Chapter 20

The Curriculum

Three centuries ago there were people in England who wanted the freedom to worship as they chose. They came to the New World as pilgrims and founded what was to become, a century later, the United States of America.

Their reason for leaving England was that the burden of tradition there made it difficult for them to establish themselves in a new identity. Probably, their difficulty sprang not only from the persecution they endured there, but also from the fact that it is never easy to begin a new life so long as a person remains surrounded by old ways of living and thinking.

Jesus remarked that a prophet has no honor in his own country. It says much for his own greatness that it didn't occur to him to add that a prophet has a hard time being a prophet in his own country.

Young people with new dreams usually must leave home to realize their ambitions. Fritz Kreisler, the famous violinist, left Austria to pursue his mission of music in America. His mother tried to prevent him from going so far away from home. Years later he remarked, "If I had listened to my mother, I would never have become Fritz Kreisler."

Change is seldom easy, even under the most favorable of circumstances. A century after the arrival of the pilgrim fathers in America, the colonies were prospering, but it became increasingly evident that the freedom which the pilgrims had sought, and which remained the dream of subsequent immigrants, required a clearer definition still. For a new spirit was growing here, one that could not flourish so long as the New World remained merely a colony.

It is not surprising that England felt threatened by this new spirit, and tried to suppress it. By its long-established standards, much of what was going on in the colonies amounted to treachery. But the simple fact was that America needed a self-identity. Only after those old traditions had been repudiated by means of the American Revolution (labeled in England, of course, the American Rebellion), and new traditions established by the American Constitution, could the new spirit attain its real place in history. New ideas demanded an entirely new context in which to flourish. In the old context, the sheer weight of tradition was suffocating them.

Obviously, where the ideas contained in this book are concerned, no major revolution is anticipated. Nevertheless, some thought must be given to placing them in a new context. It may be that they will take root only in an altogether new system of schooling.

One such school, or rather group of schools, is already in existence. It will be described in the next chapter.

It would of course be a happy denouement if these ideas were to win acceptance directly into the present school system. In such a case, however, the ground would need to be prepared for receiving them. One step in this process would be the adoption of a new curriculum of studies.

The Problem with Transplants

The present school curriculum in American schools might be adapted to the ideas in this book. Unfortunately, it is more likely that any such adaptation would resemble a heart transplant that the body's cells treat as alien, and therefore reject. Traditional categories would tend almost inevitably to reassume old definitions, in time. The Sciences, Mathematics, Social Science, Languages, and the Humanities would slowly close their gates against this brash upstart, the "Education for Life" system. It would be easier, certainly, to adapt the "Education for Life" system to the usual curriculum than to impose a radical transformation on the old system. Perhaps all that is needed is a redefinition of already-accepted categories, and not a total restructuring of them.

Indeed, any education worthy of the name must teach children the basics of modern knowledge. These basics include all of the above categories of the curriculum. Perhaps the changes I've proposed can be incorporated into that curriculum, with only a new designation for each category. There is, in fact, no need to abandon the curriculum itself, nor even to change it drastically.

America, similarly, needed only to be redefined as a country instead of as "the American colonies"—and carefully so defined, too, through its Constitution—for it fully to assume its destined role.

Here, then, are suggestions for a new curriculum—workable, I think, even within the present system. Be it noted that this proposed curriculum includes all of the standard academic subjects. The main difference is that it defines them in such a way as to invite, rather than merely to tolerate, the inclusion of creative "Education for Life" principles.

"Our Earth—Our Universe"

"The Sciences"—one of the standard categories of study—is a lifeless designation, surely. It is words without poetry, music without melody. It conjures up images of test tubes in a laboratory rather than the wonders of nature.

What about creating a new definition of this category, naming it: "Our Earth—Our Universe"? This name would cover everything that is now being taught under the arid name "The Sciences," but it would include also a suggestion of the orderliness of the universe; an appreciation for the ecological balance of planetary life; a sense of awe before the universal mysteries which, as Einstein said, is the essence of great scientific discovery.

This designation would invite the students to relate harmoniously to the universe—to feel themselves a part of everything, instead of being merely intellectual observers of whatever goes on around them.

"Our Earth—Our Universe" would suggest a progressively expansive view of reality. It would encourage students to think of the universe as a wholeness—to see the particular and the universal in relation to one another. It might even suggest a comparison between physical laws and higher principles. Newton's law of motion, for example, might suggest laws of action and reaction on other levels of reality. Gravity and electro-magnetism might be examined for their possible connection to subtler kinds of magnetism—even, if the teacher dares take the step, to such high principles as divine love. In one way or another, in any case, this subject might suggest a view of the universe itself not as something inert, but as pulsating with life. Thus, from a mere catalogue of facts, "Our Earth—Our Universe" could make of the sciences themselves, customarily the most intellectual of studies, something heartfelt and inspiring. For those interested in pursuing further my ideas on this subject—too detailed for inclusion in this volume—I suggest reading my book, *Crises in Modern Thought*.

The separate sciences, too, might be taught not only as compartmentalized disciplines, but as a totality revealed in its different aspects. Thus, nature would assume for the student an over-all coherence that would conduce toward the basic goal of education itself: maturity. It is easier, after all, to relate to diverse realities if they are seen in meaningful relationship to one another, and finally to the student himself.

"Our Earth—Our Universe" as a general heading would include the specific subjects: physics, astronomy, chemistry, biology, general science, botany, geology, and anatomy.

"Personal Development"

The subjects under the heading "Personal Development" would cover a wide range, from physical development to mental and spiritual development.

Physical development would include hygiene, diet, sex education, sports, and general physical education.

Mental development would include lessons and exercises in concentration, problem solving, how to develop the memory, secrets of balanced living, how to achieve and maintain inner centeredness, self-control, and joyful self-discipline.

Spiritual development would include secrets of happiness, and instruction in such attitudes as openness of heart and mind, truthfulness, non-attachment, calmness of feeling, willingness, servicefulness, and humility. It would also include such spiritual practices as affirmation, visualization, and meditation.

"Self-Expression and Communication"

This third category would include teachings such as mathematics and grammar, which could each be shown as a means of helping one to achieve mental clarity.

Included here would also be such subjects as how to develop creativity, and how to be differently creative in a variety of fields. Subjects might include the arts, interpretive dancing, music composition, music interpretation, and creative writing, and also instruction in how to develop more mundane, but perennially useful, skills such as carpentry, computer technology, public speaking, and salesmanship (to suggest merely a broad sampling of studies).

Students of self-expression should be taught the laws of success, and the difference between true success and the "flash-in-the-pan" popularity which so often leads to disappointment.

They should be taught the importance of the human voice as a medium of self-expression; how to use the voice to maximum effectiveness when speaking or singing; how to develop its tones, and its emotional overtones; how to project the voice as a vehicle for one's thoughts and feelings, and how to project it outward to a large audience.

Above all, the children should be taught self-expression as a means of communication, that they not think of it merely as a means of imposing their own views on others.

"Understanding People"

The category "Understanding People" would include history, geography, psychology, a study of the customs and beliefs of different cultures, and an evaluation of the mores of those cultures in relation to what human beings themselves, everywhere, most deeply want from life.

History taught in this way would be automatically expanded beyond the usual naming and memorizing of dates and abstract events, enumerated as though the story of mankind were only a matter of statistics.

Geography taught in this way would emphasize the influence on cultural development of such things as climate, history, language, challenges met and overcome, the prosperity or poverty of a people, religion, geographical location (whether insular or continental, mountainous or plain, fertile or arid). By placing these subjects in the context of "Understanding People," teachers would find it easier to hold their students' interest, since, to use an analogy, the first thing most people will look for in a photograph in which they figure is—themselves!

Psychology has too long been taught with a clinical emphasis on abnormal psychology. It is time to stand back and ask ourselves more practical and immediate questions: What do normal people want from life? How effectively do they pursue the search for fulfillment and happiness? What works best for them? What doesn't work at all? This subject has endless ramifications; the main point to suggest is that the approach be immediate and practical in terms of the students' own interests and desires.

Sociology could be taught with less emphasis on statistical findings, and more—as in my proposal for psychology—on human interest: on what movements and developments have worked best for people, and why; on a discussion of the relative effectiveness of leadership to spontaneous mass awakening; on the fact that revolutionary changes usually arise out of small, dedicated groups, and the effectiveness of small minorities, therefore, in bringing about great changes in society.

"Cooperation"

The fifth general category is named "Cooperation" in order to give a positive emphasis to subjects that are normally studied with insufficient reference to their human realities: languages, political science, economics, business.

Included here might be courses in such immediately helpful subjects as how to win friends and influence people (the title of Dale Carnegie's book); how to get along with others; how to find a suitable mate; secrets of a happy marriage; how to raise children;

how to find a job; the importance of working with others rather than against them; the art of supportive leadership; and how to develop personal magnetism.

Languages taught under the heading of Cooperation would introduce children to the important concept of learning language as a means of *communication*—of talking with *people* rather than approaching language as an abstract intellectual exercise; of listening to and absorbing the nuances of language, that it become a sharing of more than ideas. Language might be placed equally well under the category, "Self-Expression and Communication." I have suggested including it under "Cooperation" only to emphasize the sharing aspect of this form of communication. I've put the remaining subjects under this heading for the same reason.

Political Science, for example. This subject can be, and has been, studied from a Machiavellian standpoint by those who equate politics with power, manipulation, and control over others. Students of the Education for Life system should be helped to see that using anybody for one's own ends inevitably leads to one's own downfall, eventually. Nor is giving people what they want—or think they want—sufficient for successful governance. There must also, and above all, be cooperation with truth, with higher law. Political science, bereft of emphasis on cooperation, can easily degenerate into a study in cynicism. The same is true also for the remaining subjects in this category.

Economics may seem the least promising topic for inclusion under the heading "Cooperation." I place it here to help give it a new emphasis, minimizing those aspects that have won it notoriety as "the dismal science," and highlighting the opportunity for economics to be serviceful to human needs, and creative also, if only in the sense of facilitating creativity and not obstructing it.

The same point may be made with regard to business. Business should be conducted, as Paramhansa Yogananda often said, as a service to others. Only thus can it have an expansive, not a contractive, influence on the ego.

"Wholeness"

Thus, we have five subjects, four of them (Personal Development, Self-Expression and Communication, Understanding People, and Cooperation) specifically directed toward Education for Life principles, and the fifth (Our Earth—Our Universe) named in such a way as to be compatible with these principles.

There remains the need for one over-all subject with which to tie the other five together and give coherence to the entire system.

The above subjects might be compared to the spokes of a wheel, radiating outward from a central hub in humanity itself. Whatever one thinks of the saying that the most suitable study for mankind is man himself, it must be admitted universally that human nature is a focus from which no human being can escape, no matter how expansive his intentions. From our very ability to understand springs our every perception of the universe. The most distant galaxy manifests itself to our awareness only because man himself has first looked, and tried to understand what he sees. His understanding of everything defines him as he himself is. Another species, or another civilization, might behold in that very galaxy realities that have not yet so far occurred to any astronomer.

The relevance of every subject should be seen in the context of human needs and of our own ability to understand. Every subject studied in school should be studied also for its relevance to other subjects.

Science, for example, has evolved a method that can provide a new tool for understanding in all the branches of knowledge. For these other studies, the scientific method—hypothesis tested by experiment— needs only be restated as *belief tested by experience.* In essence, the two formulae are the same.

Whereas recognition might be given in all the fields to the relevance of any particular study to other studies, such recognition would have to be more or less superficial. In history class, for example, the teacher might strive to point out the relation between history and the development of artistic expression, but the central focus even so would be on history, not on art. In biology class, there might be an attempt to show the relationship between biology and the political slogan of "survival of the fittest," but the focus would have to be primarily on biology.

The benefit of Wholeness as a subject in itself, then, would be that all the other disciplines could be viewed from a standpoint of their focus in the central hub of humanity.

Under "Wholeness" would come such general topics as art and music appreciation, literature, philosophy, and religion. Spiritual development itself would come under Personal Development, but the study of religion could include a broader and more objective slant on how religion ties in with human and social needs, generally.

In teaching these subjects, constant reference should be made to the subjects studied under other headings. Thus, instruction in them will become instantly real and practical, and not merely, as is so often the case in traditional schools, abstract.

Art, music, and literature could be shown in their relation to humanity's search for perfection, and not given only an esthetic connotation. The question of good vs. bad esthetics could be expanded beyond such questions as beauty or realism to ask: What does all this mean in terms of what you and I hope for from life? is what these artists express meaningful to our own deepest needs? and if so, in what way?

Philosophy could be taught from two points of view: first, as a love for wisdom (from the Greek *philos,* meaning love, and *sophia,* wisdom), and therefore a teaching that is more theoretical and abstract; and second, as inviting the actual attainment of wisdom, and what it means, in practical human terms, to be wise.

Religion could be taught on many different levels. Suffice it here to say that the teaching of this subject should expand the student's mind beyond mere differences of belief to include the effect of religion on humanity. Similarities in the great religions should be stressed, rather than the differences. The social, historic, and human needs addressed by the founders of those religions should be emphasized, as well as the eternal need of all souls to realize themselves in their relationship to high realities. It could be pointed out that, in every religion, the usually unspoken goals are not very different, one from another.

"Wholeness" could emphasize the interrelationship between body and mind, and the importance of developing both in the quest for maturity.

"Wholeness," finally, could teach students how to achieve perfect self-integration, and the relationship between inner integration and the individual's ability to act and interact effectively with others.

Chapter 21

Ananda Schools

The system of education suggested in this book is more than a proposal: It is also a report on an actual development in our times. Many of the ideas contained in these pages have been refined in practice over several decades, including nearly thirty years of experience in a group of schools, from pre-school to high school, called the Ananda Schools.

The Ananda school system is out of its infancy, but it is still small. Its growth has been kept organic, for which reason the Ananda schools have never been widely publicized. Still, it has received steadily increasing recognition in educational circles.

Not long ago, a couple in Illinois inquired of several organizations in the eastern states of America whether they knew of a school that taught the art of living along with the standard curriculum. More than one organization replied that, for this purpose, the best school was Ananda School, near Nevada City, California.

Another couple in Florida made a similar inquiry, and received the same reply.

At Ananda schools, in other words, many of the principles suggested in this book have been practiced for years and are becoming increasingly understood. Their effectiveness has to a great extent been tested and proved.

A number of the ideas suggested in this book, however, in keeping with the principle of organic growth, are still being worked toward at Ananda schools also. What I have sought to do in these pages is re-evaluate what we are trying to accomplish, and to see whether our directions might be crystallized into a clear and coherent system called for the first time with the publication of this book, "Education for Life."

This book addresses also the broader issue of education in America, with a view to exploring ways in which the presently established system in this country might be improved.

I mentioned earlier that it has fallen to my lot to found a community. This community was begun in 1968, nearly thirty years ago. It is the larger entity of which Ananda School is a part. The community and the school both bear the same name: Ananda.

Ananda, a Sanskrit word, means Joy. Miraculously, the Ananda community has actually managed to live up to its name, and is known far and wide—internationally as well as domestically—as a joyful community. Ananda Village, with its various subsidiaries, numbers at present some eight hundred members, all of whom are dedicated to exploring and living by the principles that are implicit in an education for life.

Ananda communities are far-flung. In California there are three: near Nevada City, in Sacramento, and in Palo Alto and Mountain View. There is a thriving community near Portland, Oregon, and a fifth in Washington, near Seattle. There is also a very active community and retreat center near Assisi, Italy. Ananda schools flourish in several of these Ananda communities, notably near Nevada City and in Palo Alto, California. The original and largest of these communities, Ananda Village, near Nevada City, is situated on 700 acres in the foothills of the Sierra Nevada mountains of northern California.

Ananda Village is in fact, as its name implies, a village, not a commune. Its members live for the most part separately, in their own homes. Some own their own businesses and employ other members. Others work in businesses that are owned by the community.

Ananda School is an integral part of the community's life. It is attended not only by the community's over one hundred children, but also by day and boarding students from the outside.

The goal of Ananda School is to teach children the art of living, while giving them, in addition, the knowledge imparted by a conventional education. The principles taught here have been worked out by trial and error on the part of the teachers as well as of the children.

Existing, as Ananda Village does, outside the mainstream of city and suburban life (this is not the case with most of our branch communities), in no way implies a rejection of the society of which we are a part. Spatial removal has, however, enabled us to approach many contemporary problems in society with a fresh and creative outlook—even as the early pilgrim fathers did when they emigrated to the New World. What we have sought, and continue to seek, are answers that will be relevant to society as whole, and not only to ourselves.

Our approach, then, has been positive, not negatively reactive. While we have withdrawn to some extent from the bustle of what people may define as modern life, we have never alienated ourselves from the modern quest for growth and self-discovery. We believe in the underlying goodness of man, as we believe in our own underlying goodness. And we began from the outset with confidence that it would be possible, by devoting ourselves creatively to the art of living, to find new and useful solutions to many of society's ills. Nor has our confidence been misplaced. What we have found are, we believe, ways by which people everywhere can learn to live together constructively and harmoniously, in happiness.

Ananda School was founded soon after our beginnings in response to the needs of the children in our growing community. We were fortunate from the start to have a few state-accredited teachers.

Accreditation in many professions, in fact, has long been one of Ananda's strengths. Community members presently include a considerable number of professional people with high standing in their own fields. Our problem, at first, was not so much how to create a school, but how to approach education afresh, from a standpoint of the art of living. None of us was satisfied with the presently accepted standards of education.

Studies were made by Ananda teachers of various progressive systems of education. We weren't committed to any dogma of education, but only to finding what would work best. Much of the groundwork for our efforts, however, was done in Ranchi, India, early in this century by the great spiritual teacher, Paramhansa Yogananda. Inspired by his efforts, we committed ourselves, with him, to the premise that a growing child needs to learn *how to live* in this world, and not merely how to find and hold a job. He or she needs to know how to live wisely, happily, and successfully according to his own deep inner needs, and not to meet life with the expectation that money and a nice home will give him all that he really wants in life.

We were also eager to learn from anyone who could teach us. All the systems we studied, however, apart from the seminal ideas presented by Yogananda, struck us as incomplete. Gradually, direct experience provided us with a clarity of our own. Life itself superseded books as our teacher.

It was important to validate our evolving "Education for Life" system on level of standard academics as well. Our children needed to be able to compete adequately with children elsewhere in the country.

In fact, in nationwide exams Ananda children have tested on an average two years ahead of their own age levels. Their main qualification, however, has always been their maturity compared to children elsewhere, even compared to children considerably older than themselves. When Ananda children graduate from our schools and enter the public high school system, they are perceived by their peers as outstanding human beings.

Recently, during the graduation award ceremonies at a local high school, the award for the Most Inspiring Athlete was withheld to the end.

The coach, before giving this award, made an unusual speech, of which the following is a paraphrase: "When Michael first entered this school as a freshman, I have to admit I didn't really like him. Nor did I want to work with him.

"Then he went away for a year to study in a private school. When he came back for his junior and senior years, the change in him was tremendous—so much so that, of all our athletes, he quickly stood out as the most inspiring. Four years ago, it wouldn't have entered my mind that, someday, I'd be giving Michael this Most Inspiring Athlete award. Now I feel honored to bestow it on him."

Michael's grades, also, had shown a dramatic improvement after his return to the high school.

The private school he'd attended during his sophomore year was Ananda School.* (He remained there only one year, because, he said, he felt a need to return and "make good" in the school where, initially, he'd done so badly.)

Well over a thousand adults in the United States and in Canada have taken courses in what was originally called our "How-to-Live" system of education. One of the teachers for this course was Michael Deranja, who helped to develop Ananda's system of education from its beginnings.

In Deranja's experience with the Ananda children, his salient characteristics from the start were the humility to learn from them also in return, and the compassion to help them each according to their individual needs. Without this unusual blend of humility, compassion, and, of course, competence, it is doubtful whether the "Education for Life" system presented here could ever have come into being.

An example of compassion in our schools may be seen in the case of Sandy, a girl who studied at Ananda from the fourth through the eighth grades. When she arrived, her dislike for arithmetic was so strong that any effort to interest her in it would set her sobbing.

Instead of forcing her, Deranja tried to win her gently, by slow degrees. By the time she left Ananda School, arithmetic—of all subjects!—had become her

---

* Ananda School used to include a high school. The program may soon be re-instituted.

favorite. It remained so throughout her high school years. At the time of high school graduation, when Deranja last saw her, she told him that her dream was to become an accountant.

Compassion has helped to evolve a system that is not dogmatic, and not theoretical, but soundly practical.

The remaining question, in considering the living expression of this "Education for Life" system at Ananda, is whether such a system could be made to work in schools everywhere. And the answer needs to be as down-to-earth in its practicality as the system itself. For though most people, perhaps, would like to see at least some of these principles included in the normal school curriculum, we mustn't blind ourselves to certain realities: the vastness of the system, and, to be accepted into it, the necessity for compromise.

An elephant is harder to push than a mouse. Exxon, the largest company in the world, had to spend fifty million dollars merely to change its American name from Esso to Exxon. "The establishment," whether in business, politics, or education, is called that precisely because it is established—entrenched, in fact, in a habit structure perhaps too massive for even a revolution to alter it drastically. Even minor changes would require disproportionately vast outputs of energy.

I think we must resign ourselves to seeing these "Education for Life" principles accepted only gradually, if at all, into the already-established system, and very probably not during my, or even your, lifetime. Delayed acceptance, however, need not cause discouragement. Such, simply, are life's realities. If even a few children are helped, moreover, the contribution of this system will have been substantial.

I am reminded here of something Buckminster Fuller once said. He was in his eighties, and almost at the end of his life. A radio interviewer asked him, "Don't you get discouraged sometimes, talking and writing so much to promote your ideas, but finding so few people willing to accept them?"

"Not at all," Fuller replied with perfect equanimity. "New ideas always require at least one generation to become accepted. I know I won't live to see my ideas fulfilled. But I'm confident that they will be accepted, by future generations."

Probably, the proposals in this book will only gain acceptance, at first, in private schools, and in relatively small ones at that. Perhaps, indeed, it will be years before they are fully accepted beyond the Ananda school system itself. No doubt it will be better this way, too. It will assure the system of a clear and unimpeded head start. From these beginnings, the system may then reach out gradually to other schools, and enter the public system only after decades, if at all. The impact of these ideas, however, will, I think, be much more immediate. It is in this way that new ideas often enter the main stream—as though from underground, hardly noticed except perhaps as a new freshness in the feel of the water.

The great German physicist Max Planck (as I wrote earlier) commented wryly that a new scientific concept gains acceptance not so much because of its logical persuasiveness as because the old generation of scientists dies out, and a new generation grows up that is familiar with the idea.

The important thing to realize is that problems encountered in the initial acceptance of these concepts in education will very likely not lie in any lack of readiness in the American psyche. Americans generally are desperately aware of the need for a change in their educational system. Rather, the problems will lie in the fact that the mechanics of the system are too cumbersome to permit easy alteration, or the rapid assimilation of new ideas.

Chapter 22

Making It Happen

An Ananda child, five years old, once accompanied her mother to a laundromat in nearby Nevada City. There, the two of them saw another woman angrily scold her little boy for some trivial peccadillo. The Ananda child turned to her mother in amazement and asked in a whisper, "Why is that mommy behaving so badly?"

I posed two questions in the last chapter that might be restated thus: First, Can the "Education for Life" system, developed in a little community near the western edge of the North American continent, prove useful to schools in the crowded mainstream of modern life? and second, How can the children raised there ever expect to relate realistically, once they grow up, to this Twentieth Century world?

In this book we have defined maturity as the ability to relate to realities other than one's own. Is it not necessary, in the light of this definition, to *test* children's ability to relate to those realities—indeed, to familiarize the children with them?

The astonishment of that Ananda child on beholding a grown woman lose her temper argues an unfamiliarity with a reality to which most Americans have become inured. Is it good, one wonders, for a child to be removed so completely from every-day, though regrettable, realities?

In short, how does a child who has been raised in an atmosphere of love and harmony handle himself when confronted suddenly with anger and disharmony? Will he not find himself at a serious disadvantage, compared with people to whom selfishness and negativity are simple facts of life?

The image comes to my mind here of someone setting out to read every book ever written in an effort to master all human knowledge. The task would, of course, be impossible. And even if it were possible, our brains were never made to assimilate such an ocean of information.

The worldly sophisticate, priding himself on the number of books he has read and the number of facts he can recall instantly to mind, can do little more than skate over the frozen surface of reality.

Maturity, defined as the ability to relate to the realities of others, doesn't necessarily imply a need to go hunting for an endless number of such realities to which to relate. The more mature an individual, in fact, the more poised he will be in himself—not selfishly, but like a wheel that is perfectly balanced at its center. The less he will be inclined, therefore, to go out in search of a fulfillment outside himself.

Maturity means, among other things, a state of inner equilibrium, in which nothing can shake one's poise. Only in such a state of balance can a person relate effectively to a wide variety of realities, however foreign they may be to his own actual experience of life.

All of us have sometimes to deal with negative emotions in ourselves. It isn't as though anger, fear, belligerence, and other human weaknesses were as foreign to us as the corona around the sun. A calm school and home atmosphere, and an education focused on raising a child to emotional maturity, make it easier for the child to deal with that negativity in himself. It isn't that his negativity is banished to non-existence. Rather, he learns to meet it with an open mind and overcome it.

Once negativity in oneself has been dealt with, rather than merely indulged in, it becomes easier to deal with it objectively in any encounters one has with others. The best way to deal with anger, for example, is not to shout back and lose one's temper, but to meet it with unshakable calmness. That person who is poised in himself is invincible. Others defer to him; often, in his presence, they shelve their anger.

I have referred in this book to expanding awareness as one of the goals of maturity. One might compare this expansion to the broad base of a pedestal. A pedestal that has a broad base cannot easily be toppled over. The more expanded a person's aware-ness, similarly, the more difficult it is for anyone or any circumstance to upset him.

And who is capable of handling himself effectively under any circumstance: the person who is easily up-set by everything? or the one who remains calm in every storm?

As Rudyard Kipling wrote:

If you can keep your head when all men round you
Are losing theirs and blaming it on you, . . .
Then you're a man, my son.

The Education for Life system taught at Ananda schools prepares children to meet challenging situa-tions in another way also. For what one expects from others is very often what one ends up receiving from them. If we doubt others' good faith, even the best of them may be tempted to justify our negative expectations of them by challenging *our* good faith. But if, on the other hand, we believe in them, even the worst of them may do what they can to justify our belief.

Kindness, good will, a spirit of cooperation, and similar positive traits, if manifested with energy, are magnetic; they usually attract from others a response in kind. Even where a positive response is not forthcoming from others, moreover, the harmful effect of a negative response on oneself is invariably minimized.

The "Education for Life" system proves its validity under the most adverse circumstances. It is practical. It is not a system for the few only—for the isolated, or the "spiritual": It is for everybody. Whether one lives in the mountains or in city slums, its principles are practicable everywhere.

The question remains: How to adopt this new system?

As we pointed out in the last chapter, it would be simplest, at first, to incorporate an "Education for Life" system into small, private schools. For it is best for those launching a new concept in education to have to deal with a minimum of entrenched attitudes.

It might even be preferable to start out afresh, with new Ananda schools. Such branches might provide the shortest distance between two points: a straight line from the idealistic intention to the practical fulfillment.

Many of the ideas in this book, however, though perhaps difficult to incorporate in their entirety into already-existing situations, might be introduced slowly—perhaps one, or just a few, at a time. Much might be accomplished, in fact, in quite a number of suburban communities, for example—especially the smaller ones—if the people living there were sufficiently desperate to embrace a change.

A visit to Ananda schools would be an obvious way to begin the process. First-hand observation is always more instructive than hearsay.

There is also another possibility: A by-product of Ananda School's administration is a team of advisors on the "Education for Life" system. One function of these advisors, known collectively as "Education for Life Associates," is to travel wherever they are invited and give classes and seminars in the principles outlined in this book, as well as to suggest ways in which these principles might be incorporated, whether wholly or in part, into other school systems.

If even a few communities in America succeed in adopting these principles, a notable start will have been made toward solving some of the deepest problems facing us in American society today.

For further information, please write to:

Education for Life Foundation
Ananda Village
14618 Tyler-Foote Road
Nevada City, CA 95959
Telephone: 916-478-7640

Afterword to the Second Edition

It has been twelve years now since J. Donald Walters wrote the first edition of Education for Life. Shortly thereafter, Mr. Walters created the Education for Life Foundation. Since its inception, this foundation has had the opportunity to create a living laboratory for the values brought forth by this book. It has provided seminars for hundreds of educators throughout the world, established three Education for Life schools, and observed the fruits of a balanced education and its effect on children. The results are proven and as convincing as the philosophy. Children who have gone through the school system have learned and practiced how to live in a positive, balanced way. Experience has shown that by giving children the tools and understanding to make right choices in life, we can lead them to lasting happiness.

The author has extensively rewritten the book for this second edition, clarifying the exposition and introducing new material that provides futher practical foundations for educators.

Crystal Clarity, Publishers

Index

Education for Life Foundation

Education for Life is a system of education that has the same goal as life itself: progressively to become on every level—heart and mind, body and spirit—more balanced, mature, effective, happy, harmonious human beings. The Education for Life Foundation applies these principals through:

Elementary and High Schools
Ananda School, Ananda Village, Nevada City, CA
Ananda School on the Peninsula, Palo Alto, CA
Ananda School Portland, Portland, OR
Sacramento School for Living, Sacramento, CA
Ananda School, Seifen/Forst, Germany

Workshops

Presenters from the Education for Life Foundation conduct in-service training for groups of teachers and parents. Seminars on the Education for Life system teach how to:

1. nurture each child's balanced development of body, mind, feelings, and will power
2. motivate all children by engaging their natural strengths and abilities
3. create a dynamic, fun, and focused learning atmosphere

4. individualize your approach to discipline and motivation while working with the whole group
5. honor your own inner life
6. expand your intuitive skills.

Other workshops offered include nurturing a child's inner life, uplifting children's literature, working with the special challenges of junior high students, and designing curriculum.

Teacher Training

Each summer the Education for Life Foundation conducts seminars. Participants have the opportunity to experience Education for Life in the classroom directly as students, as well as to learn how to implement this holistic approach in any teaching setting. Private and public school teachers, scout leaders, environmental educators, adult educators, students in traditional teacher training programs, and home-schooling parents have all found the program of great benefit.

We are always interested in hearing from educators who have incorporated these values into their school system. Please contact us with your experience and feedback at:

Education for Life Foundation
14618 Tyler-Foote Road
Nevada City, CA 95959
(916) 478-7640
E-mail: Anandaschool@efl.org
Internet website: http://www.efl.org

Resources

A Selection of Other Crystal Clarity Books
For information call **1-800-424-1055.**

Secrets of Winning People
J. Donald Walters

Each *Secrets* book is a collection of profound thoughts, one for each day of the month. Here you'll find words of wisdom for living with courage and grace, as well as warm comfort for life's inevitable ups and downs. Teachers, parents, managers, salespeople—anyone working with people will draw inspiration from this powerful book.

$5.95 . 1-56589-030-2 . 72 pages . hardcover

Secrets of Leadership
J. Donald Walters

An ideal book for those who lead, teach, or work with people. This book contains 31 secrets of leadership—wise guidance for overcoming challenging situations from the author of *The Art of Supportive Leadership* and *Education for Life.*

$5.95 . 1-56589-034-5 . 72 pages . hardcover

The Art of Supportive Leadership
J. Donald Walters

Learn how to achieve your goals, not by driving the people under you, but by supporting them. Here is a new approach, one that views leadership in terms of shared accomplishment rather than of personal advancement. Perfect for managers, teachers, parents, and anyone who leads others. Recommended by Kellogg and other corporations in their management training programs.

$7.95 . 0-916124-20-7 . 104 pages

"The Art of Supportive Leadership stands out among business books."

—Roger Griffith, Executive Book Summaries

"We have been casting about for something like this for a long time. It's especially good for new managers. Highly recommended." —Kellogg Company

Crises in Modern Thought
J. Donald Walters

The scientific advances of the last century have, in some ways, also introduced a sense of meaninglessness into modern life. As the scientific principle of relativity has become widely accepted, traditional values have been greatly weakened. *Crises in Modern Thought* shows how science and values are, in fact, completely compatible. Working with accepted scientific theories, *Crises* shows how science and the basic moral values of society enrich each other.

$11.95 . 0-916124-47-9 . 280 pages

"This is wonderful! Crises in Modern Thought *is completely in harmony with the findings of modern science. Yet it provides them with deep meaning. This message must be spread everywhere!"*

—Leon Kolb, anthropologist, Stanford Professor Emeritus

Cities of Light: What Communities Can Accomplish, and the Need for Them in Our Times

J. Donald Walters

Utopian communities can, and do, exist here on earth. *Cities of Light* describes the principles that have helped the Ananda communities to become a beautiful embodiment of spiritual ideals, as well as dynamic, supportive environments for personal growth. This book explores new concepts in living for business, relationships, marriage, the arts, education, and the home, and offers answers to the growing need for alternative ways of living in today's society.

$9.95 . 0-916124-44-4 . 134 pages

Autobiography of a Yogi

Paramhansa Yogananda

One of the great spiritual classics of this century. This is a verbatim reprinting of the original 1946 edition of *Autobiography of a Yogi*. Although subsequent reprintings, reflecting revisions made after the author's death in 1952, have sold over a million copies and have been translated into more than 19 languages, the few thousand of the original have long since disappeared into the hands of collectors. Now the 1946 edition is again available, with all its inherent power, just as the great master of yoga first presented it.

$14.95 . 1-56589-108-2 . 481 pages

A Selection of Books from Dawn Publications
For information call 1-800-545-7475.

Sharing Nature with Children
Joseph Cornell

This classic is Joseph Cornell's original collection of 42 fun nature games with clear, concise directions and fascinating descriptive stories. More than 380,000 sold in nine languages! Recommended by Boy Scouts of America, American Camping Association, National Audubon Society, and many others.

$7.95 . 0916124-14-2 . 144 pages

Sharing the Joy of Nature
Joseph Cornell

In his second book, Joseph introduces his remarkable technique of Flow Learning, showing how to match nature activities to the interest and energy levels of children. Success in any nature experience!

$9.95 . 0-916124-52-5 . 176 pages

Journey to the Heart of Nature
Joseph Cornell

Journey to the Heart of Nature guides the reader on an in-depth exploration of a personally selected part of nature. Stories from the lives of John Muir, Jim Corbett, J. Allen Boone, and many other adventurers provide a springboard for a wide variety of fascinating activities. Written specifically for young adults, this book also offers special opportunities for adults, either for personal use or as an ideal means of sharing a remarkable adventure with older children.

$9.95 . 1-883220-06-8 . 128 page